# MANAGING PEOPLE

## 25 Steps to Improving
## Employee Performance

# MANAGING PEOPLE

## 25 Steps to Improving Employee Performance

### ROBERT KENT

**SIDGWICK & JACKSON**
LONDON

First published in Great Britain in 1988
by Sidgwick & Jackson Limited
1 Tavistock Chambers, Bloomsbury Way
London WC1A 2SG

First published in the United States of America
in 1986 by Dodd, Mead and Company Inc.

ISBN 0-283-99619-6

Printed in Great Britain by
St Edmundsbury Press Limited
Bury St Edmunds, Suffolk
for Sidgwick & Jackson Limited
1 Tavistock Chambers, Bloomsbury Way,
London WC1A 2SG

# Table of Contents

# ABOUT THE AUTHOR

Robert H. Kent is the Chairman and C.E.O. of The Mansis Development Corporation, a Canadian-based consulting company that specializes in installing human resource management systems. Through Mansis, Bob lectures and consults extensively with the management of a wide variety of organizations and industries.

In addition to Mansis, Bob has held faculty appointments in several Canadian universities, teaching organizational behavior and administration in faculties of business and medicine. He has also held senior management and executive positions in many government and private corporations and serves as a director of several organizations.

Bob's academic background includes degrees in mathematics, computer science and business administration and a Ph.D. in organizational behavior from the University of British Columbia.

After earning his doctorate from the University of British Columbia, Bob continued his research in management training and development and organizational behavior. In 1977 he founded Mansis and the company rapidly grew to become one of Canada's leading developers of human resource management systems, marketing its consulting services throughout North America.

# Foreword

Here it is in plain print, step-by-step instructions to figure out why an employee isn't getting the job done.

From a decade of helping managers solve employee performance problems, we've learned that before a manager speaks to an employee about the problem and its possible causes, the manager should have some idea of what to be probing for.

We've developed a tool that gives managers guidance and direction for analyzing problems. In the time it takes you to read this book, you'll learn what it has taken specialists years of research to find out: how to diagnose the causes of employee performance problems. You'll learn the procedure without having to wade through the latest textbooks yourself. That process has been done for you.

The Problem Diagnosis Algorithm* sums up volumes of information on one piece of paper. It is your tool to analyze employee performance problems quickly and correctly for it helps you to logically structure your thought processes, gearing them for results.

Learn how to diagnose performance problems and make good decisions with economy of thought by following the steps outlined in the Problem Diagnosis Algorithm.

**Robert H. Kent, Ph.D.**
*Chairman and C.E.O.,*
*The Mansis Development Corporation.*

---

*The Problem Diagnosis Algorithm is part of the Mansis Performance Management System.

# Acknowledgements

Many people have influenced the development of this algorithm. Particularly, the works of Herbert Simon, Stan Herman, Victor Vroom, Ed Lawler, Bob Mager, Ferdinand Fournies, Ken Mac-Crimmon, Lev Landa and Ron Zemke have given me inspiration and direction.

For writing and editing assistance with this manuscript, thanks go to my wife Cathryn, many friends and associates, and especially Nadine Shannon.

# 25 STEPS

# What is an Algorithm?

An algorithm is a decision-making flow chart. The concept comes from various scientific disciplines, particularly the area of human problem solving. It's known that individuals commonly use flow charts in their minds to help them make decisions. They may do it consciously or subconsciously, using these "decision maps" that they've developed through experience. Decision-making algorithms can save time by solving recurring problems.

Research shows that algorithms play a part not only in how individuals make decisions but also in how organizations make decisions. Companies develop guidelines called "standard operating procedures" and it's these rules which determine to a great extent how the organization operates.

Research on employee training techniques shows that people learn faster and apply their knowledge sooner if the skill being taught is presented in algorithm form. With an algorithm you can teach people complex procedures in dramatically less time than it would take using more conventional teaching techniques.

It's possible to draw up an algorithm for any decision-making process once you discover the appropriate thought process. If you want to learn how to interpret financial portfolios for making investment decisions, for example, you can use an algorithm to simplify the process and learn it in hours instead of months.

## THE ALGORITHM IN ACTION

The following is an excerpt from a recent instruction manual for some personal computer software: "If you are familiar with version 2.0 of our word processor program, go right to Chapter 3, unless you have never run the program on a Macintosh computer, in which case review Chapter 2. But if you have never worked with version 2.0, start at Chapter 1, unless you have used version 1.0 of the program, in which case you can start at Chapter 2." Loses you fast, doesn't it! Here's how an algorithm handles this verbal maze:

**Instruction Manual: Where To Start**

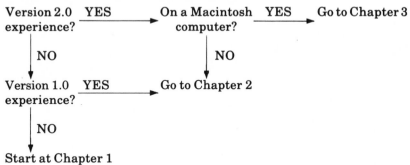

Start at Chapter 1

When managers have employee performance problems, they don't have time to learn all the relevant management theories or to investigate all the possible causes of problems. It's too complicated.

Fortunately, there's no need to learn everything and investigate all causes. You can solve problems and save time using the step-by-step approach outlined in the algorithm which follows.

# The Problem Diagnosis Algorithm

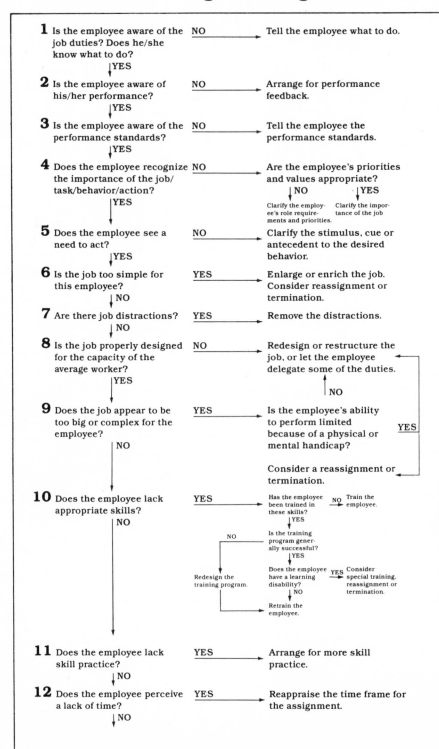

**1** Is the employee aware of the job duties? Does he/she know what to do?
NO → Tell the employee what to do.
|YES

**2** Is the employee aware of his/her performance?
NO → Arrange for performance feedback.
|YES

**3** Is the employee aware of the performance standards?
NO → Tell the employee the performance standards.
|YES

**4** Does the employee recognize the importance of the job/task/behavior/action?
NO → Are the employee's priorities and values appropriate?
|YES

      |NO       |YES

    Clarify the employee's role requirements and priorities.     Clarify the importance of the job

**5** Does the employee see a need to act?
NO → Clarify the stimulus, cue or antecedent to the desired behavior.
|YES

**6** Is the job too simple for this employee?
YES → Enlarge or enrich the job. Consider reassignment or termination.
|NO

**7** Are there job distractions?
YES → Remove the distractions.
|NO

**8** Is the job properly designed for the capacity of the average worker?
NO → Redesign or restructure the job, or let the employee delegate some of the duties.
|YES

    |NO

**9** Does the job appear to be too big or complex for the employee?
YES → Is the employee's ability to perform limited because of a physical or mental handicap?
|NO         YES

    Consider a reassignment or termination.

**10** Does the employee lack appropriate skills?
YES → Has the employee been trained in these skills? NO → Train the employee.
|NO     |YES

    NO     Is the training program generally successful?
      |YES

    Does the employee have a learning disability? YES → Consider special training, reassignment or termination.
    Redesign the training program.   |NO

    Retrain the employee.

**11** Does the employee lack skill practice?
YES → Arrange for more skill practice.
|NO

**12** Does the employee perceive a lack of time?
YES → Reappraise the time frame for the assignment.
|NO

**13** Does the employee perceive a lack of tools, equipment, materials, funds, support staff or other resources? — YES → Reappraise the resource support including materials, funds, support staff, etc.

↓ NO

**14** Is the employee's poor work being rewarded? — YES → Eliminate the inappropriate reinforcers and reinforce the good behaviors.

↓ NO

**15** Is the employee's good work being punished? Is there peer pressure against good work? — YES → Eliminate the source of punishment and reinforce the good behaviors.

↓ NO

**16** Is the employee's good work being extinguished? — YES → Start an appropriate reinforcement schedule for the employee's good behaviors.

↓ NO

**17** Did the employee misunderstand directions? — YES → Does the employee have a learning disability?

↓ NO ..... ↓ NO ..... ↓ YES

Re-explain directions and ensure two-way communication. ..... Compensate for learning disability or consider a reassignment or termination.

↓

**18** Did the employee forget to do the job? — YES → Act according to the seriousness of the issue. Try a mechanical solution.

↓ NO

**19** Was the poor work simply a matter of human error? — YES →

↓ NO

**20** Was the poor work a result of the employee's personal problems (health, family, finances)? — YES → Evaluate the problems and coach or counsel accordingly. Consider professional assistance.

↓ NO

**21** Is the employee insecure, lacking self-esteem or confidence? — YES → Reappraise your relationship with the employee, and coach the employee.

↓ NO

**22** Is there a personality conflict? — YES → Translate "personality" problem into a "behavior" problem, and resolve.

↓ NO

**23** Does the employee distrust the company, co-workers or you, especially regarding receiving rewards for his/her good performance? — YES → Clarify misunderstandings and expectations.

↓ NO

**24** Is the employee apathetic, unconcerned? — YES → Increase the employee's motivation, and coach, or discipline.

↓ NO

**25** If you've been through steps 1 to 24, then you're probably being led down the garden path. Forget diagnosing the reasons and just enforce the performance standards. Consider discipline.

# The Problem Diagnosis Algorithm

The Problem Diagnosis Algorithm is an easy-to-use decision aid having two main advantages: it presents managers with the conclusions of decades of complicated research summarized on a single page; and it structures a manager's thought processes economically so that the more common causes of employee performance problems can be investigated first.

Two major concepts influenced the development of the Problem Diagnosis Algorithm.

## 1. THE KISS TECHNIQUE OF MANAGEMENT

One of the best rules of thumb for management is the K.I.S.S. technique — Keep It Simple Stupid. If you can put thirty years' research into a simple chart, do it. So that's what we've done. We believe in developing management tools that are practical, techniques people can use that clearly show "how to do it."

## 2. THE ONION-SKIN APPROACH TO PROBLEM DIAGNOSIS

When an onion is cut in half, all the different layers are visible. If we let the onion represent performance problems, each layer then represents a probable cause. The layers on the outside represent the common and simple causes with the easiest resolutions. The layers at the core of the onion represent the more complex and less common causes. These deeper problems aren't easy to solve.

In order to discover the cause of a problem we should peel away one layer at a time. It's more efficient and often more correct to avoid jumping to conclusions by burrowing right to the core. If you're in the habit of looking deep into the "onion" as soon as you detect a performance problem, you're presuming the problem is deep-seated, for example, a psychological problem of motivation or attitude, or a problem of poor organizational design.

Certainly, it's far more exciting to look to the core of the onion — that's the really sexy stuff — but rather than presuming the problem is at the center of the onion, start at the outer layer and strip away one layer at a time. It may not seem as exciting at first, but it's more effective. It lets you avoid the common mistake of making more of a performance problem than it really is and as a result coming up with expensive, elaborate, overkill solutions that usually don't work. By assessing the simplest causes first, you often solve the problem sooner.

What you'll be doing to an extent is making use of Pareto's mathematical law, the 80/20 rule. Applied to this situation, it's likely that 80 per cent of employee performance problems are caused by 20 per cent of the probable causes. Likewise, about 80 per cent of probable causes are related to only 20 per cent of the problems.

Since the majority of problems are caused by a small set of causes, you can be economical with your time by ruling out those causes first. This algorithm enables you to do that because it directs you through the outer layers, the common causes, first.

Over the last decade, my associates and I have helped thousands of managers and hundreds of companies identify and solve employee performance problems. From practical experience, we know what works and what doesn't work. When it comes to reasons for poor work, we've heard them all and the algorithm attempts to take them all into account.

# How To Use The Algorithm

The purpose of the algorithm isn't to discover that a problem exists. You already know that. The purpose is to help you find the cause and then to provide you with a course of action to remedy the problem.

Before you look for a cause, be clear in your mind what the performance problem is. Is the employee insubordinate? Clowning around? Showing up late for work? Doing poor work and not measuring up to performance expectations and standards? Be as specific as possible about the nature of the poor performance. What is the person *doing* that you don't like?

As well, be clear about what you want the person to *do*. Don't say "pick up your socks," or "smarten up," or "your work had better improve," if what you really want is to have sales increase by ten per cent or you want the employee to be on time for all meetings or to stop telling jokes in the office.

Before confronting the employee with the facts, give some thought to possible causes of the problem. In some cases the employee may know why he or she isn't performing well and may be able to propose a suitable solution. That's ideal. The solution will be theirs and it's more likely to be implemented if that's the case.

It may be though that the employee is not aware of either the problem or the cause. Rather than you dictating a solution, it is better if the two of you can discuss the problem and, with your guidance, the employee is able to develop a solution himself. You can aid in this process if you are aware of the probable cause yourself.

If you don't know the cause of the performance problem, start the algorithm at question number one and progress through the chart. After you're familiar with the algorithm, investigate whichever of the causes you first suspect could be causing the performance problem. Knowing the algorithm will make you more aware of the range of causes and will give you an appreciation of the most common ones.

## THE ALGORITHM ISN'T DOGMA

The algorithm is a guideline. It's not intended as dogma and it is not a formula to live or die by. If you can improve it by your own experience, by all means do so. Your experience with employee performance problems is as valid as anyone else's. And if you do adjust this algorithm slightly for your particular needs, let me know of your changes. I'd welcome comments about your experience.

# STEP 1

## What Am I Supposed To Do?

Is the employee aware of the job duties? Does he/she know what to do? → **NO** → Tell the employee what to do.

Does the employee know what to do? Is he or she aware of the job duties? These questions are asked first because the number one cause of performance problems in all industry is people not knowing what to do.

The boss presumes that the employee understands what the various tasks and duties of the job are. It's a common assumption. Yet a great many employees, whether they're just beginning their jobs or receiving recognition for ten years of service, do not know what their job duties are.

To avoid making this assumption yourself, put new employees through a systematic orientation program. Include explanations of job duties; guidelines as to the authority that goes with the job; a rundown of company policies, benefits and safety practices; and anything else that will help to clarify what the job is and what you expect in the way of employee performance.

### ORIENTATION AS A MANAGEMENT TOOL

An employee orientation program is one of the best methods for preventing most employee performance problems. It also strengthens morale. Yet many organizations do not provide any systematic employee orientation. Instead, they spend vast sums of money recruiting and selecting employees, then let those who are new to a job learn the ropes through trial and error. It doesn't make sense! The results are obvious — costly mistakes, frustration and negative attitudes toward the job and the organization. Perhaps orienting an employee to a new job is so obvious it's overlooked. Or maybe it's dropped along with other job teaching programs in order to cut costs.

Because ignorance of job duties is such a widespread problem, it's been looked at by a number of organizations. The federal government of Canada, for instance, did its own survey a few years ago. The results showed that 30 per cent of all federal government managers did not know their job duties. (At today's salaries, this represents over $300 million.) Another 30 per cent didn't find out the details until after they'd been in their jobs for one year, via a bad performance appraisal rating. It follows that more than $300 million tax dollars were spent to support activities over which taxpayers had no control.

I find the situation worse in the private sector. Unlikely? Well, at least with government bureaucracies, there's formal documentation on the duties and responsibilities of a particular job. In the private sector, there usually isn't much bureaucratic documentation. People step into their jobs with little or no formal instruction.

In one company, for example, a man was given an interim promotion from foreman to plant manager for a major production plant. His instructions were short and sweet. "You're in charge now." His boss assumed he'd figure out how to do his job and that somehow he'd find out what his duties were. Of course, that didn't happen. He failed at fulfilling his duties and was criticized for not doing the job properly.

Another typical example was the new head of the social service agency. She was selected because of her professional credentials as a counsellor and her aspirations for a "new improved" agency. Her directions from the board of directors were to "run a smooth ship" and "it's in your hands now, do whatever has to be done." Ten months later she was fired. It seems she thought she had more authority than board members wished and she never did what was really expected.

This problem does not have to happen. You can "solve" it before it ever occurs by making sure your employee is oriented to the new position and at the very least has a job description.

## JOB DESCRIPTIONS
## CENTRAL TO GOOD MANAGEMENT

For many of us, job descriptions smack of bureaucratic administrivia. But whether you run a huge manufacturing business, a small clothing store or a rural school, the job description is your primary document for managing people. It's fundamental for all aspects of personnel management and the courts are now saying it's important for all levels in an organization.

The job description serves many purposes. When we recruit and select a new employee, we have to make sure that our selection decision is based on criteria related to the actual job that the new employee is expected to do. For this purpose, we need an accurate job description. A sketchy promotional outline designed to attract candidates isn't sufficient.

Besides being useful for employee selection, job descriptions also relate to performance appraisals. Appraisals must be based only on the employee's performance in his or her job, no more, no less. In the absence of a formal legal employment contract, the job description becomes the contract and the performance appraisal serves as a measure of how the contract was met. To judge by any measurement other than the job description is unfair.

A job description is also an important document in termination. If you fire someone for not fulfilling the requirements of his or her job, make sure you have something in writing outlining what the job requirements were. And make sure the employee gets a copy, not when he's fired but when he's hired.

Every supervisor has to be prepared to give an explicit answer to the following two questions about each employee: "What does this person have to do in this job to make me happy?" and "What would I fire him for doing or not doing?" Put these questions to yourself as an aid in building a job description. As soon as you've answered them and told each employee, you'll be managing better.

### FORMAL OR INFORMAL?

I am not saying you must without exception hand over a formal job description to your employees for every position in your company. The uses for highly detailed and formal documentation are usually more related to salary classification.

Usually, managers will groan out loud if anyone mentions

"job descriptions." They feel that giving an employee a job description will limit their own flexibility in assigning tasks to that employee. They're afraid that their employees might work to rule. Certainly some of their fears are justifiable. But remember, if you are paying a person to do a job, it makes great sense to tell the person what the job is. The job description needn't be overly complex and detailed nor should it take hours to write, but you must tell the employee what is expected.

The amount of detail you give will naturally vary according to the seniority of the position. Your senior vice-president of administration doesn't need to be told how to prepare an annual budget (perhaps), but she certainly deserves to know that you expect the budget on your desk by next Monday. Make it clear what's expected.

If you hired a player for your football team, you'd make certain your player knew what position he was playing. And you'd be sure to let him know what the duties of that position were. No coach says, "You figure it out. Play ball." Instead, the player is told what plays work well. He learns how to play with the other members of the team and he's coached to reach an understanding of how his job (or position) functions in relation to the whole operation. His coach may well say, "Go out there and win." But the coach will also tell his player to run to the left when the quarterback drops back for a particular play. The player is given enough details to be able to play the game in a way that will satisfy the coach.

## GET IT IN BLACK AND WHITE

Putting the job description down on paper helps you make sure the message is clear and therefore helps prevent misunderstandings. Your words aren't cast in cement, though. Job descriptions can be changed as your needs change and as the job evolves.

You may decide to hire a specialist to write up job descriptions — many people do turn to specialists to avoid this task — but don't put off telling the employee what to do while you decide which specialist to bring in. Many companies get around to bringing in consultants once every ten years. As a result, the whole process of communicating job expectations becomes constipated. Your employees can't wait ten years to learn what their jobs are and you can't afford to pay $30,000 or even $3,000 for a position over which you have no control.

## DON'T IGNORE THE HIGHER UPS

Surely, you might say, the senior executive doesn't need to be told what to do, doesn't need to have the boss say profit is in and losses are out this year. Well, in fact, senior management is the level most in need of communication about job duties. It's a cop-out for a president to say to a vice-president, "It's your job to tell me what your job is."

# HERMAN®

## "What are you asking me for?"

## MANAGEMENT BY DROPPING HINTS

There's a common management style I'm discovering among presidents and senior executives. I call it management by dropping hints.

I hear executives saying things like, "I don't understand why Smigelski's not doing her job — I've dropped enough hints." Or, "Why doesn't Frigelbum take the hint? I want him to give me a once-a-month written report on client calls so that I'll know exactly how successful he is compared to previous months. Whenever I ask him how his calls are going he says everything is fine but I know for a fact he's making fewer calls." The president feels it's a personal affront to have to verbalize expectations.

Presidents who manage by dropping hints sometimes devise little tests to see if their executives can read their minds. And they present these tests to people for whom they're prepared to pay $60,000 to $90,000 a year!

Why do managers "manage" by dropping hints? Perhaps it's due to personality traits, or possibly these managers have never seen managing done any differently so they think that that's the way to do it. Or maybe it's just not clear in their minds what they want subordinates to do.

Other managers may take too much for granted and assume too much. They may assume what's common sense for them (given their goals and their objectives) is common sense for the other person. Or, managers may be so involved in what they perceive to be their own problems that they feel they don't have enough time to be telling other people what to do.

As a manager though, you should separate your employee's ability to do the job from her ability to read your mind. It's a shame that so many employees fail at their jobs not because they couldn't do the job, but because they couldn't read the boss's mind. Give your employees a clear indication of what you expect from them and if they don't know what to do, tell them.

---

### SUMMARY POINTS
- Don't manage by dropping hints. Develop job descriptions for all employees and be explicit about what you want done.
- Don't expect employees to read your mind. Tell them what you want.

# STEP 2

## So How Am I Doing?

| Is the employee aware of his/her performance? | NO $\longrightarrow$ | Arrange for performance feedback. |
|---|---|---|

Employees may know *what* they're supposed to be doing. What they may not know is how *well* they are doing it. Paul, the high school janitor, might not be aware of the results of his work. Suppose he's doing poor work, leaving pools of water in the hallway after he's mopped up or forgetting to empty the waste bins in the staff rooms. Yet all along he's assumed that his work has been satisfactory since no one said it wasn't. If this corresponds to one of your employees and the person is not aware of his performance, then it's up to you to let him know.

### ARRANGE FOR PERFORMANCE FEEDBACK

It's common for people to be working diligently at their jobs, breezily completing this assignment and that, unaware of the fact that they're not meeting performance standards. For example, John, a secretary in a typing pool, may type up letters and habitually make mistakes. He's not aware of his mistakes for when he types up a letter incorrectly, it goes to his manager who says, "Good grief, John did this all wrong. We won't give it to him to type again; we'll give it to Susan. She types letter perfect and it's got to be done in a hurry." So the letter goes to Susan. Susan types it up correctly and the letter goes back to the manager. Meanwhile, John never learns that the letter was done incorrectly. He's presumed his work is fine because it's been accepted. Because of a lack of performance feedback, he never learns that what he's been doing isn't acceptable and consequently his poor performance continues.

To make sure a person such as this typist knows how he is doing, he should be involved in monitoring his performance. Incorrect work should be returned to him. He shouldn't be dependent upon someone else's initiative to provide feedback by an indirect route.

## PROBLEMS FROM LACK OF FEEDBACK

Failure to provide performance feedback mechanisms can sometimes cause serious problems. A classic case which recently happened in a major urban center illustrates the need for performance feedback. A woman in her late seventies fell in the street and hurt her leg. That day, she went to an emergency department of a nearby hospital. The attending physician diagnosed a bruise with minor abrasions and told her to go home and stay off her feet. The pain got worse.

She then went to the emergency department of another local hospital. The attending physician said it was a sprained hip. She was to take a hot bath, take some aspirin and rest in bed. She did what she was advised but still the pain persisted.

She went to a third hospital. For some reason, the attending physician decided her condition warranted an X-ray. The X-ray showed a fracture. At her age this could be permanently crippling and possibly fatal. So she was put in a cast from stem to gudgeon.

Unfortunately there wasn't any performance feedback for the first two physicians to learn about their incorrect diagnoses. Since the woman never returned to them for further care, presumably their diagnosis was correct. Yet they had "learned wrong." And because no one told them, they could make similar mistakes in the future. The problem was not that the doctors weren't bright or conscientious but that there was no feedback mechanism to inform them of performance results.

Other examples of "learning wrong" come from the university setting. It's a rare day indeed when a university student gets to see a graded final examination. Grades are given out but the student can't be sure which answers merited the marks. An accounting student could write a final exam, get a passing grade and set up office the next day, remaining uncertain of where the knowledge was missing. My family physician had a 95 per cent average and graduated from medical school as a gold medalist. I just hope I never go to him with an ailment in the 5 per cent region he doesn't know about, because he doesn't know he doesn't know what he doesn't know. In fact, he probably doesn't know that he does know what he thinks he doesn't know!

The reasons for giving performance feedback are solid ones. If your employee is not aware of her performance, tell her how her performance rates and where improvement is necessary.

## DOCUMENT EMPLOYEE PERFORMANCE

Get it down on paper. Write up an objective, factual account of what the employee has done on the job.

Documentation doesn't mean recording just bad performance. A manager should be aware of all the employee's behavior — work that is being done well and work that needs to be improved. A useful technique is to create an incident file or anecdotal record. But a word of caution. All too often the anecdotal file contains all the instances of less than satisfactory work and rarely the instances of good performance. Most anecdotal records end up being reservoirs of only the bad because the employee's good work is to be expected and therefore no note is made of it. Whenever less than adequate work is done — pop — into the file it goes, and we end up building a lop-sided assessment.

What also happens regularly is that we try to build a factual account of behavior only when we need to discipline or dismiss someone. We scramble to document a case against some ne'er-do-well, trying to recall the employee's history of bad work and jotting down everything in defence of a feared grievance or law suit. Unfortunately our efforts are usually too late. An employee can rarely be disciplined effectively based on the boss's vague recollection that, "She was late on a number of occasions, as I recall."

Memory, of course, does act like a file, even if you don't keep official files on your employees. The trouble is, it's quite natural to remember the bad behavior and forget the good. Bosses make a mental note when employees do something wrong or forget to do an important part of an assignment. Yet often they won't make a mental note of the good, standard, satisfactory performance because it's simply expected. "That's her job."

Since memories don't keep an accurate record of employee performance, it's a good idea to set up your own working file for every individual for whom you're held accountable. This file doesn't have to be the official personnel file used for union/management purposes or for official discipline or dismissal. It's simply your working file. Use it to keep track of performance for the people you manage.

## WHAT GOES IN THE FILE?

Include all written correspondence between you and your employee. You may also want to keep a record of personal things like birthdays and maybe the employee's children's names and ages. That's entirely up to you.

Remember that as soon as you create a file on an employee, the employee has the right to see what's in that file. In fact, the employee should review the files with you regularly.

With whatever else you put in the file, put in two more pieces of paper. These are going to become your employee Performance Profiles. Here's a way to set them up. Spend about fifteen minutes, maybe in an evening after work, and think about one of your employees — Elizabeth, for one. Sit down and give some thought to what Elizabeth does well, things that you're pleased with and that you wish she'd keep doing. These don't have to be spectacular events, but just the good, satisfactory performances with which you're quite pleased. List these on one sheet of paper and call this page "Satisfactory Performance." What you list are *behaviors*, things that the individual *does*. To pinpoint an employee's behavior, you define it in such a way that anyone listening to your description could see the behavior, or count the behavior. As well, describe the situation in which the behavior occurs.

If your organization has a performance appraisal form, what are the factors or categories on which you will be expected to rate people at year end? What is the employee now doing related to each of these evaluation factors? Use these factors as your guide to identifying behaviors to list on the Performance Profiles.

On your other sheet of paper, list behaviors that you want to see changed or improved or stopped. Call this page "Performance Needing Improvement."

## KEEP YOUR RECORDS CURRENT

Discuss with each employee what you've initially recorded. From then on, perhaps monthly, add examples to this record to keep it current. Many managers who use this approach invite the employees to contribute examples of their own to the record.

Unless you're keeping some record of what each employee is doing, good or bad, you really can't be on top of the situation and you can't claim to be managing employee performance. The files give you a snapshot of each employee's performance at a particular moment and recording the full spectrum of performance enables you to reinforce good work as well as confront and change the bad. When used effectively, this ongoing track record can be used to ensure productivity, to nip performance problems in the bud, to motivate the employee and to develop an accurate and balanced data base for yearly performance appraisals.

Giving frequent feedback to the employee is crucial for good performance. There is no value in performance records kept secret or discussed only at yearly performance appraisal interviews. Courts will not uphold dismissals or discipline based on records undisclosed to the offending employee.

The basic principles of performance documentation are making sure that all of your employees know at all times how well they're performing and making sure they know that you are aware of their performance. There should be no secrets. Everyone should know at all times where he or she stands with the boss.

---

### SUMMARY POINTS
- Performance feedback is a continuous process not an annual event.
- Create recording procedures so that the employee is continuously aware of how well the job is being done.
- Don't let anecdotal records become reservoirs of only the bad.

# STEP 3

## Is This Good Enough?

Is the employee aware of the performance standards? — NO → Tell the employee the performance standards.

People commonly are not aware of what the difference is between excellent work, average work and poor work. They either don't know what the performance standards are, they don't know how the standards apply to them, or else the performance standards themselves aren't explicit. They are often told to "pull up their socks" or "smarten up!" The end result is that employees don't know what standards to work toward.

It's your responsibility as manager to see that your employees achieve the performance levels you plan for. Therefore, it's your responsibility to tell employees what the standards are. There's a bonus to doing this. When you let employees know explicitly what excellent work is, they will more often give you that quality of work.

In the Social Sciences, one of the most consistent research findings is that when employees are given clear, measurable performance goals and standards, their work performance improves for no other reason than the target was made clear. The employees weren't paid more money, they weren't trained more or motivated more, nor did they have more or better equipment. They achieved a higher level of performance simply because they knew what they were striving toward.

As a rule, managers do not tell their employees what the

performance standards are. Many managers don't know themselves; they haven't given it much thought.

There's a flurry of literature now in the popular press about "excellence" in management. The underlying message is that managers and companies should strive for excellence in order to survive free market competition. But while companies are sincerely taking this message to heart, most have difficulty stating clearly what excellence means to them. How is "excellence" to be operationalized?

## HOW TO CLARIFY PERFORMANCE TARGETS

Making your employees' performance targets clear involves two steps: establishing the levels of performance your employees should be shooting for, and communicating to the employees what they have to do to reach the target.

Setting the target is likely to be the tougher of the two jobs. However, you might decide without much fuss that your auto mechanic should be able to install four new mufflers a day in addition to serving three hours at the service desk. That's one performance standard for your mechanic. But for some types of jobs, such as research and executive positions, it's difficult to quantify performance standards with the same degree of clarity. It will take some extra thought. In any case, the boss ultimately has to be able to answer the question, "What will I be pleased with?" If you're the boss and you can't answer that then you must be willing to accept any performance standard as a satisfactory one. Under such circumstances you're not managing your employees; they are self-managed and can't be held accountable for their performance.

## SETTING UP BAR SCALES

For the majority of positions, we can make performance standards very clear. One way is to develop behaviorally-anchored rating scales (BARS). To do this formally, you first spend lots of time and money collecting critical incidents of job behavior and then do mathematical gymnastics to come up with some very sophisticated rating scales. Instead of taking this route, I recommend the following:

1. Determine the categories for which you want to measure employee performance (or use the categories on your organization's performance appraisal form if you have one).

2. Identify examples of typical job behavior you'd expect to see employees perform to earn a low, medium and high rating on each category. You could even involve your employees in identifying typical job behaviors that are unacceptable, average or outstanding.
3. Use this rating scale, anchored in behavior, to guide employees away from inappropriate behavior and toward the specific type of performance you want.

It is important to include only behaviors that are relevant to the job and essential to success on the job. To illustrate what not to include, here are some characteristics and traits that often show up on appraisal forms: attitude, personality, loyalty, initiative, output, dependability, people-orientation, appearance, reliability, cooperation, enthusiasm and maturity. Unsupported by a behavioral definition, these terms more properly belong off the record as they are too vague and different managers and supervisors interpret them differently.

Where measurement criteria in a performance appraisal can be defined differently by different managers, the criteria are said to be unreliable and should not be used. Imagine your confusion if your boss told you one day, "I don't like your attitude. Sure, you're doing your work well enough, but I don't think you're very loyal. You ought to show more maturity when you're at work and take initiative a little more than you do. You've got two weeks to show some reliability or I'll have to consider letting you go." There are better ways to appraise performance.

## USING BEHAVIORALLY-ANCHORED RATING SCALES

Here's an example of a performance appraisal rating that has been "anchored" in behavior using a Behaviorally-Anchored Rating Scale. In this example, the manager is defining for the employee what she considers to be relevant behaviors for each point in the scale. You may not agree with the manager's definition of initiative, but at least the employee is aware of what the boss is looking for. "One" represents the lowest and "four" the highest rating on the scale.

### Factor Name: *Initiative*

**Performance Level One**
Employee refuses to perform any activities assigned by the manager if the activities are not spelled out in a job description.

Employee often says, "I don't have to do that — you can't make me do that."

### Performance Level Two
Employee frequently complains and argues when assigned extra work. However, the employee usually does the work, although reluctantly.

### Performance Level Three
Employee cheerfully accepts any extra work assigned by the manager.

### Performance Level Four
Employee asks the manager for additional work to do when there is slack time. The employee seeks out opportunities to help the department perform its activities.

Here's another example.

## Factor Name: *Typing Correspondence*

### Performance Level One
Correspondence typed with errors more than 3 times/month. Proofreading not always done. Typing submitted late more than 3 times/month. Corporate letter format not used at all times.

### Performance Level Two
Occasional failure to catch errors when proofreading — 1 to 3 per month. Typing completed at last second leaving no time for last minute changes.

### Performance Level Three
All correspondence error free when mailed. When given assignments, completed by prearranged deadlines.

### Performance Level Four
By using word processor, all correspondence leaving the office is letter perfect, no corrections necessary. Typing is completed well within deadline leaving time for unexpected changes. Typist catches and corrects grammatical errors made by writer. Anticipated correspondence and routine letters are prepared, without instruction, in advance.

In your own BARS, stick with a scale of one to four, indicating low to high, and give your employees some clear examples of what you expect to hear or see in order for them to score a "four." The more examples the better. Remember, people want to succeed and most will try their hardest to score a "four."

You will also have to define the other three points on your scale with behavioral examples. This gives each employee an idea of what is not expected and which behaviors are to be avoided.

For those employees who score low, be sure that you communicate to them that they're doing poor work. If they're kept in the dark, you are being unfair. Managers are responsible for making it clear exactly what the employees should be shooting for and for doing whatever they can to help the employees reach their set performance goals. And when people reach those goals, when they achieve a "four" rating on the BARS, be sure to reward them with a "four" rating. Don't hand out a "three." This is no time to be stingy. Even if all your employees perform at the highest level on the scale, recognize their performance and give them all "fours." You can always set higher standards next year.

Managers who take responsibility for directing their employees to high performance levels are good leaders. Research findings show that successful leaders are the ones who are able to create well-defined and acceptable goals for their employees. They are the ones who make sure there's a clear path to proceed along toward those goals, that is, that employees have what they need to reach the goals: skills, self confidence, and necessary resources. A clear path also implies that obstacles such as red tape and distractions have been removed.

## HOW MANY POINTS ARE
## NEEDED ON A RATING SCALE?

Four are sufficient. To have a rating of one to ten (or more!) on a rating scale is meaningless. Most human performance and job behavior can't be split into so many degrees of performance. What's the difference between an "eight" and a "nine," or a "six" and a "seven?" Having a top level of four gives ample range for recording degrees of effectiveness.

I strongly object to the use of a ten-point (or similarly high number) rating scale. It's been my experience that companies using a ten-point system get caught playing games with their employees.

## TWO MYTHS ABOUT
## SCALES AND PERFORMANCE APPRAISALS

*Myth One*
"We don't give 'tens' at our company because that suggests that you're perfect. Nobody's perfect."

It's a myth that on a performance rating scale the top level means perfection. It doesn't, or at least it shouldn't. Of course no one is perfect. But the highest point is not equivalent to perfection. It's unrealistic to say it is.

The top level on your scale is the highest point that is achievable. If it isn't achievable, it will tend to demotivate your employees. If there is some point representing "perfection", it shouldn't be on your scale at all.

*Myth Two*
"We can't give our employees a 'ten' because then they'd have nothing to strive for next year."

"Having nothing left to strive for" is a myth because when most employees reach their goals, they try to reach them again. But to never award the highest score on the assumption that the person wouldn't try to achieve it again the next year is poor policy and unsupported by experience.

It's not true that people who do well one year won't strive to do well the next. How many children who got "A's" in grade two arithmetic said, "There's no more challenge here," and promptly quit striving for the top performance level? Likely none. They kept striving to get more "A's."

It's our nature to strive for the top even if others have been there before us. Carl Lewis didn't mind getting four gold medals just because somebody else achieved that before him. However, it's unlikely that athletes would compete enthusiastically in the Olympics if the gold medals were withheld so that athletes would have something left to aim for next time.

If someone does perform at the top level, don't be afraid to make your top end more challenging for the next year. If some of your salespeople are consistently bringing in ten per cent over budgeted sales, give them recognition and then negotiate to raise your performance levels next time.

## A WORD OF CAUTION
## ABOUT PERFORMANCE FEEDBACK
Don't expect employees to jump for joy because you've decided to level with them and tell it like it is. No matter how objective, valid and supportive this feedback might be, you're going to find some, and possibly many, who are overly defensive, rejecting any performance critique, hostile or retreating into a shell.

Ironically it's frequently the lack of valid, timely, job-related performance feedback that makes people overly defensive. And management reacts to this overdefensiveness by giving even less feedback. The overdefensiveness becomes self-perpetuating.

The only way to stop this vicious circle is to start giving feedback that is job related, timely and objective. But expect initial rejection and distrust. Such reactions are predictable, but usually short lived.

Many performance appraisal programs have failed because management wouldn't hang in long enough to tough it out, to get through the defensiveness that had grown over the years.

---

### SUMMARY POINTS
- Develop clear behaviorally-based performance standards for all performance categories that you rate employees on.
- Make sure that all performance standards are achievable.
- Give an employee a top rating when it's earned.
- Expect some defensiveness and rejection when a performance feedback system is first implemented.

# STEP 4

## It's Not That Important!

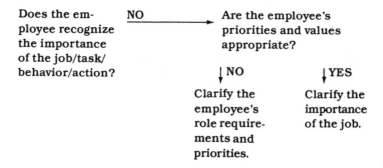

Does the employee recognize the importance of the job/task/behavior/action? — NO → Are the employee's priorities and values appropriate?

↓ NO — Clarify the employee's role requirements and priorities.

↓ YES — Clarify the importance of the job.

Sometimes jobs aren't completed or started or done as well as they could be, simply because the employee didn't think the job was important.

The employee knew it ought to be done but for some reason it was low on her priority list. "I knew you wanted me to do it eventually," she might respond, "but I didn't think it was that important." And that could be the reason why it wasn't done. Perhaps the employee didn't know what the priorities were for the job, which things were more important than others, and therefore did not recognize the importance of the job.

Failure to recognize the importance of a task can explain an endless list of performance problems such as:

-omitting to lock up an office or file cabinet

-typing correspondence that isn't letter perfect

-overspending a budget

-neglecting staff training and development

-infrequent or delinquent submissions of sales reports, cash flow reports, month-end statements, etc.

-failing to make sales follow-up calls or to return telephone
 calls
-spending too much time on trivial job responsibilities
-being one of the gang and too close to the employees

## THE CONCEPT OF ROLE

When you talk about priorities in a job, you're essentially talking about the concept of role. Is the employee aware of the
role he or she is supposed to play in the position held? If the
employee isn't aware of what tasks should be done first, then the
manager's job is to clarify the role requirements and priorities.

When people step into new jobs, they're usually given some
idea of what the job activities are. Possibly they've been given a
job description outlining some of the things they're supposed
to do. But job activities only form a part of the employee's role.

The concept of a role comes from the theatre. Suppose you
were going to act in a Shakespearean play and play the role of
Macbeth. To throw yourself into the role, you'd do more than
simply memorize the words and learn where to stand on stage.
You'd learn how Macbeth would interact with other members
of the cast and you'd learn or try to understand the values or
priorities that the character Macbeth would have. As well, what
sorts of relationships would Macbeth have with the other char-
acters? How would he interact with them? You'd investigate this
so you could play the character as Shakespeare had intended.

We can begin to understand management and employee
relations better if we understand the roles we have to play
as managers or as employees. This involves clarifying the
components for each role.

A role is comprised of a set of expectations, values, relationships and activities that is associated with a position. Role
has less to do with the position holder than it has to do with
the position itself.

## ROLE EXPECTATIONS

Because of the position you're in, what are the things that are
expected of you by your boss, by your peers and by your subordinates? Also, what do you expect of each of them?

Many times people will carry out their job activities but
they'll fail in the eyes of their subordinates or in the eyes of the

boss because they didn't meet expectations. Yet frequently those expectations were never communicated. The boss assumed the person would know what they were. Remember the manager who just drops hints? That manager hasn't learned how to identify and communicate role expectations.

## ROLE VALUES/PRIORITIES

What values should you have in order to carry out the requirements of your role? What should you be placing value on? Values have a direct effect on the decisions you make. Although the word "values" is difficult to define, the appropriate values for a position can nonetheless be clarified by talking about the priorities for the position. Which things are more important than others? What you should be saying to employees is, "Look, this is the most important thing for you to do, this is the next most important thing, and so on. I want you to place priority on this item."

Values and priorities are inherent to all types of jobs. To clarify the appropriate ones, it comes down to this: if your employee has a choice between two activities, give some guidance as to what should be done first. If you leave it up to your employee to decide, then you're taking the risk that the job may not be carried out the way you want it done. Knowing the priorities of a job is part of knowing the job itself.

Certain tasks are usually more important than others, yet rarely are these priorities ever pointed out in a job description. Which is more important, quality or quantity of work, work done perfectly or work done on time? Everything can't be top priority.

A problem I find in many companies involves one typist typing for five or six managers. Everybody gets upset because work isn't done on time. Yet, often the problem arises because the typist hasn't been given priorities. Does Job A have to be done right now or can it wait a week? Everyone claims his or her work is priority number one, but in all likelihood it doesn't have to be. Clarify the priorities that go with a position and you're going to do away with a lot of common employee performance problems.

It's hard to rank everything a person does in a job, but it can be done. To put job tasks in priority order, make a list of the main things an employee does. Decide which is the most important and which is the least important. Eliminate these two tasks from the list and write them down at the top or bottom of another list. Of those items remaining on the original list, which is the most important task and which is the least? Add these next items to the new list at the appropriate position. Continuing in this manner, you can build a ranked list from most to least important and help your employee set priorities for job activities.

Another example of priority problems occurs when an employee moves up into management but doesn't adjust his or her priorities to suit the new "role". For example, the priorities or values of a ward nurse's role would include giving the best direct patient care possible, and giving precedence to patients' interests and problems. However, once that nurse is promoted to head nurse and manager of the department (usually because she was such a good nurse) her priorities need to change because her role has. Now her priorities should be giving the best patient care possible within a budget, controlling costs wherever possible, and providing high quality patient care through a well-trained and motivated staff. Her former values don't disappear but they may take second place to these new ones.

But what often happens? No one told the new head nurse that her values or priorities should be adjusted and nurse role values are probably very close to her own personal values because that's what motivated her to enter nursing in the first place. As a result she gets ulcers from the natural conflict between budget restraints and giving the best nursing care possible. Instead of developing her staff to give excellent care, whenever problems arise with a patient, she rolls up her sleeves and says to her staff, "Stand aside, I'll take it from here." Her priorities and values motivate her to give hands-on treatment, consequently her staff is never properly developed and becomes demotivated because "she never lets us do our job."

## IS THE CULTURE TO BLAME?

This problem may not be a result.of just the employee's misperception of the "appropriate" values. It could be that the organization's or the department's values, reflected in work norms, are inappropriate and counterproductive to the goals of the organization. And it's these organizational norms that may be influencing the employee and causing problems. In a nut shell, the organization's culture is to blame.

The impact of organizational values, norms and rules of thumb on job performance ("the way we do things around here") is easily overlooked especially by senior managers who are frequently buffered from what is really going on, down on the line. The result is that efforts starting from the top of the organization to implement change, give new direction and get the job done, frequently fail when they meet a resisting culture.

For example, take the case of the company president who sincerely wants all his employees to participate in problem solving and in generating new ideas. He encourages an open door policy and insists that lower management regularly consult employees to solicit ideas, problems and solutions. "Show initiative" is the president's motto. Although reports to the president from his personnel director indicate that managers have been trained in soliciting ideas from staff and that many brainstorming and problem solving meetings have been held, the reality is otherwise.

Most employees of this company don't offer any ideas let alone identify work problems. The few who do, do so with great hesitancy and suspicion. Why? Because the norms in the company are "protect your backside", and "don't raise problems or you'll just have more work dumped on you". The organization's culture is not one of integrity. Feedback is not honest and political self-centered games abound. But the organization dutifully supplies the "objective" data to let the president feel good about the illusion of participation.

My experience is that information directed upward to senior management is severely filtered by the organization's culture and norms. As a result many executives and corporate directors appear to accept on faith, that the values they expect their organizations to hold actually influence the work force behavior.

Another example of divergent values is in manufacturing. Corporate mottos, posters, public relations campaigns and pep-talks all stress quality production. Executives preach quality to the work force and pledge quality to the public. But on the assembly line, the work values and norms don't reflect quality at all. "Push the product through as fast as possible or there'll be hell to pay. Ignore mistakes and errors — it'll probably be recalled anyway." Novice employees soon lose their naïveté and learn the facts of life on the production line.

The solution to an inappropriate corporate culture is beyond the scope of this book, but suffice it to say that all too often senior management is not as aware as it should be of the organization's norms and values in practice; nor does management take the necessary measures to see that organizational behavior reflects the desired norms and values.

## ROLE RELATIONSHIPS

To carry out the demands of your managerial position, whom should you have working relationships with and what sort of working relationships should they be? There are many types of working relationships and the key is to ensure that you and your employees develop the appropriate relationships with the right people.

Relationships is an area where many problems arise for new managers. Sometimes priorities are put on the wrong relationships. Suppose you are new to management and you rose from the ranks. Before moving up there were peer relationships between you and your fellow workers and there was a boss-subordinate relationship between you and your boss.

The peer relationships were close ones and you knew the people quite well. They were the gang you went out and socialized with. The boss-subordinate relationship was also straightforward. The boss had the right to give assignments and to tell you what to do within the confines of the job. You expected your boss to be impartial in judging your performance and in letting you know how well you did your job.

But when you enter management, life becomes a lot more complicated. Suddenly you're the boss. You have the authority to tell others what to do and you have the responsibility to judge the performance of others. Literally overnight you have to develop a boss/subordinate relationship with people you had a peer relationship with yesterday.

It's difficult to establish new relationships and change old ones. Not everyone does it successfully. Many get their new management roles mixed up with their old non-management roles and become too distant or too familiar. Take Carol, for example. It seems that she rarely speaks to her old friends any more. Or how about Hank now that he is a boss? He pretends he's still one of the gang. He drinks with the guys and mixes in at office activities. He wants to be your friend but then he uses that friendship to stick you with heavy workloads. Or else he lets old-you-know-who get away with murder, sloppy work and haphazard attendance because they're such close buddies.

It's very common for new managers to continue playing the former non-management role, forgetting the age-old rule — you can't be one of the gang and be an effective boss. You say to yourself, "It's the same old me. It's the same old gang. Just because I'm doing a different job there's really no reason for not working with the gang like I did before." And of course your former peers often agree. "Come on, knock off the boss stuff. Why don't you just be yourself?"

It's appropriate to attend the staff parties, but not to social- ize all evening and close the doors! After all, the staff is also evaluating you and you have to develop a sociability but not an overfamiliarity. Although you're the same person, your role has changed. Now you have to lead the team. You have to discipline, hire, fire and perform other tasks that demand objectivity. Objectivity and impartiality will be suspect if you're one of the gang and it's got nothing to do with what you say or do. It's what others choose to hear or see! Like Carol, you'll find yourself having to change old peer friendships. Sad to say, that's one of the prices to pay for promotion into management, especially if you become the boss of your former work mates.

## ACTIVITIES

Job activities make up the final part of the role. Job activities are the tasks you perform in your position. Activities should be spelled out in your job description. Possibly they're noted in your organization's operating procedures. If job activities aren't covered in writing, and all too often they aren't, then confusion and misunderstanding can take place.

## ROLE CLARITY IS ESSENTIAL

A lack of clarity in any of these four areas — expectations, values, relationships, activities — can result in role ambiguity and role conflict.

Role ambiguity happens when the employee doesn't know what his role is. He's not sure what's expected of him and he isn't sure what he can expect from other people. He doesn't know what values he should have. He doesn't know what sort of working relationships he should have and with whom, and commonly, he isn't sure of what he's supposed to be doing in the job. Ambiguity also can result when he's not sure of his authority or job responsibilities. These latter insecurities could be caused by a lack of orientation when he entered the job, poor communication from the boss or simply poor organization.

A lot of research is showing that when the role is ambig- uous to the individual, the result is low job satisfaction, low self-confidence, a lot of tension and stress on the job and a sense of futility. Eventually, keeping people in the dark about their role leads to poor performance.

Role conflict arises because in our lives we play multiple roles. We may be playing the role of boss in one instance and subordinate in another. But what may happen is that elements of these roles conflict — the expectations may conflict, there may be contradictions, values may differ and activities may demand differing priorities. For example, in some organizations the front-line managers are also members of the union. On the one hand, they are expected to play the role of management and hold management values. On the other hand, they are members of the union and of course there are going to be values associated with that role. This brings about obvious role conflict that can lead to problems on the job. In addition there can be conflict between other components of the role — relationships, expectations, activities. Such conflict can often result in low job satisfaction, low confidence in the organization — the individual feels the organization has put him in an impossible situation — high tension and stress.

A common example of role conflict occurs when a manager has a best friend working for him. He plays the role of the friend, with the close relationship that entails, and he also plays the role of the boss, which requires a more distant relationship.

We're never going to avoid having some role conflict in life and we may have to change hats as we go from role to role. But as managers, we must be aware of the potential for role ambiguity and role conflict in our employees if they work under uncertainty or with contradictory demands.

## ARE THE EMPLOYEE'S
## PRIORITIES AND VALUES APPROPRIATE?

Is the employee putting emphasis on the wrong parts of her work? When this happens, it's your responsibility to clarify priorities for that employee. Instead of stomping on her because she didn't recognize job priorities, it makes more sense to tell her what the priorities are. Don't expect her to read your mind.

What if she has the job priorities right but doesn't recognize the importance of the task? Well, maybe in her opinion, the job wasn't important. Maybe she didn't associate this particular job with the priority job. Your job as the manager is to simply say, "Yes, this job has to be done." Let her know why and clarify the importance of the job.

## SUMMARY POINTS

- Clarify role expectations between you and your boss and especially your employees.

- Prioritize your employee's job responsibilities and activities. Everything can't be number one.

- Cultivate and insure the appropriate work relationships between you and your employees. Don't become too distant or too close. Don't be one of the gang.

# STEP 5

## There Was No Need To!

| Does the em-<br>ployee see a need<br>to act? | NO           ⟶ | Clarify the<br>stimulus,<br>cue or<br>antecedent<br>to the<br>desired<br>behavior. |
|---|---|---|

Maybe the employee knows what's to be done, knows how to do it and knows it's important that the job be done. And maybe he fully intends to do the job at the appropriate time. But perhaps he just doesn't recognize the appropriate time. He doesn't see that there is in fact a need to do the job right now. So the job isn't done.

Suppose an employee of yours needs to learn how to delegate work. You send him to a course where he can learn how. He completes the course and comes back to work. He now knows both the importance of delegating and how to delegate. But he never does it. Six months after the course, you've yet to see him delegate one assignment to anyone. So you start giving him heck because he isn't using the skills he's got. "Well, sure, I can delegate, boss," he says, "but I didn't see the occasion when I could have delegated." He's quite sincere about that. Everything was going fine, so why delegate? "My workload wasn't horrendous. I was managing to get through a day's work. There was no need to delegate." It's an instance where the person didn't recognize when he should be delegating.

## HOW TO CLARIFY THE CUE

If the employee doesn't see a need to act then clarify the stimulus, cue or antecedent to the desired behavior. Make it clear to employees what should precede particular activities. Let them know when to perform those activities. For example, what happening or event should stimulate that employee to delegate? How will he know, "Hey, it's time to delegate." You could say, "Look, whenever you're performing some activity that somebody working for you and getting paid less could do just as well, consider delegating. That's not the only time you'd delegate, of course. You also delegate assignments that are simple or repetitive or delegate in order to develop your subordinates' skills. You don't wait until you're swamped with work to delegate; you delegate as a development technique."

## THE IMPORTANCE OF BEING CLEAR

Suppose, though, that your employee works with mechanical instruments and on occasion fails to follow instructions. Again, ask yourself the question, "Did the employee see the need to act?" Perhaps he is supposed to shut down a machine when the dial reaches a certain point. He might know that when things get really bad, "I'm supposed to shut it down because it might explode." But how does he know exactly when to shut down the machine? "Nobody told me that when the dial reached one hundred I was to shut it down. All I was told was to turn off the machine if it looked as if it might explode." Someone forgot to let him know how to recognize when it is important to act.

On a personal level, have you ever driven on a freeway in a strange city looking for a specific turnoff? Remember how it felt when your navigator announced "Here's the turnoff!", the very instant you roared by at seventy miles per hour in the wrong lane? Announcing the turnoff that precedes the one you want would make it clear that the time has come to prepare to exit from the freeway. Such cues should be prearranged.

## THE STIMULUS FOR PERFORMANCE FEEDBACK

The use of performance appraisals offers another example of how important it is to clarify the stimulus for desired behavior. Lip service is paid to the value of giving performance feedback since it's obviously a good idea. Bosses expect to get around to giving appraisals eventually but they don't see the need for appraisals now because so far everyone is doing a good job. They don't see a need to act and aren't aware of when they're supposed to give feedback. What often happens is that performance feedback is given only when things go wrong. More appropriately, feedback should be given when an employee is performing well.

Some municipalities are now prevented by court rulings from retiring employees at age sixty or sixty-five as long as performance is acceptable. This scuttles the practice of using retirement to eliminate alleged unproductive employees. Consequently some politicians and administrators grab on to performance appraisal as a means of firing people, and implement performance appraisal implicitly for this reason. Unfortunately, this sends powerful negative messages throughout the municipal workforce and the failure to recognize that performance appraisal has a positive role to play becomes institutionalized.

The famous old line from the boss, "Unless I'm giving you *! *?!, you know you're doing good work" is a classic example of how not to manage people. The boss recognizes the value of feedback, but the cue he uses for giving feedback is any time when things are going wrong. As a result, the boss and the employee interact only when the employee is being given  *! *?!. The boss isn't aware that the need to give performance feedback should follow all kinds of situations.

Your role as boss is to direct and lead your employees to perform appropriate work behaviors. By helping employees recognize what precedes the behaviors you want them to show, you'll be able to solve a lot of seemingly complex employee performance problems.

---

### SUMMARY POINTS
- Make sure employees know *when* specific activities or behaviors are to be performed.

# STEP 6
## What a Bore!

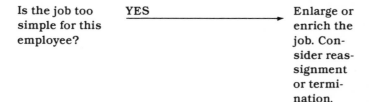

| Is the job too simple for this employee? | YES ⟶ | Enlarge or enrich the job. Consider reassignment or termination. |
|---|---|---|

Maybe your employee is listless and prone to fooling around because he's bored. Either the job is too simple or he's too bright. There is no challenge and no intrinsic satisfaction from doing the work. This means you have to change the job to stimulate the employee or relocate him in a more appropriate job. Next time, make a better match between the job and an employee's aptitude and aspirations.

## SOME JOBS ARE JUST BORING
Some jobs consist of short-cycle, repetitive, simple tasks that seem to go on forever — sorting or delivering mail, filing, typing, operating a telephone switchboard, most clerical functions, proofreading and verifying, assembly line activities and more. In a few days the job is learned and top performance levels can be consistently achieved. Many of these jobs are like perpetual motion machines — no beginning, no end. The employee can never experience a sense of accomplishment because nothing of significance is ever completed. With the increased levels of education and aspiration in today's labor force, jobs like these won't keep employees content for long, especially considering

the simplistic level of decision making required. Matching words and numbers or making simple muscular movements becomes the sum total of these jobs.

Perhaps only this particular employee finds the job boring; other employees do not. He learns very quickly and is able to perform the job so well that he surpasses the job requirements in a flash. He's hungry for more stimulating work but it's not there. His perception is, "Hey, this job isn't me. I can do better," and his mind is looking elsewhere, often into the future.

## MAKE THE JOB MORE STIMULATING

One solution is to "enlarge" the job. This means putting more and different activities into the job. If Fred can sort and deliver all the mail on time for two floors, maybe he can handle another floor too. Susan handles accounts payable for the office in a breeze. Let her update the inventory records and do mail lists as well. Maybe she could gather data on suppliers for the survey you always wanted to undertake.

Another solution, sometimes more satisfying to the individual, is to "enrich" the job. Instead of just adding more things to do, put more authority into the job. Have the person make more decisions and take more responsibility for a broader part of the work. So, for Fred the mailboy, let him determine his own pick-up and delivery schedule and give him authority to classify and process outgoing mail and expedite registered and courier deliveries. As for Susan, she might be taught to handle more complex accounting functions, to prepare monthly statements or to interact personally with creditors and negotiate better terms for payment. Some automobile assembly line operations have achieved better productivity when a team of workers moves through the assembly process building the complete automobile, rather than standing at stations continuously performing the same over-specialized activities.

The degree of enrichment is limited only by your imagination and the skills of the employee. Of course this may require paying a little more salary. But even so, increased productivity and morale should easily justify any salary increase. People often thrive and grow on realistic challenges and accomplishments.

## PUT GOALS INTO A JOB

For those jobs that never have an end to them, why not build in some short-term goals — measurable conclusions to activity?

This allows employees to experience some achievement, no matter how minor, and in a psychological sense at least, celebrate a success.

For example, in a bottling department of a distillery, each assembly line crew competes with previous crews for the number of bottles filled, labeled and packed with no breakage during the shift. Whenever a crew sets a new record (which is frequent) the crew foreman goes to the nearby bank and purchases a silver dollar for each person working that shift. Employees covet these one dollar awards and rec rooms are frequently adorned with such success symbols.

At a zinc smelter, what was once a hard, boring, repetitious and unpopular job became one of the most sought after positions when the company built a goal into the job. Rows of large copper plates are suspended by a pulley system in an enormous zinc bath the size of a football field. Electricity draws the zinc out of the solution onto these plates. The employee's job is to raise these zinc-coated plates and move them by the pulley system to a location where the pure zinc is knocked off the plates. Then each clean plate is returned and lowered back into the bath. Repetitious, dull, hot and hard work with no end to it! It was hard to get people to stay in the job let alone work steadily. Then management determined that one good day's work would equal cleaning three rows of plates. This was instituted as the daily performance goal. If an employee reached this goal before the end of the shift, he would get paid for one full shift and allowed to go home. Young, strong, summer students could "run" the job and complete the goal in less than four hours, then take the rest of the day off or get another job. Older employees could pace themselves, fully aware of the daily goal. Thus the most unpopular job became very popular and absenteeism and turnover almost disappeared.

A basic challenge for management is to create goals like these for repetitious jobs. What mini-goals could a typist, clerk, receptionist or assembly line worker strive toward, to increase satisfaction, sense of accomplishment and feelings of personal growth? Perhaps as a goal you might consider reaching specific performance levels for a period of time, or the completion of a project such as typing a complete study or mailing out an edition of a newsletter.

## MAYBE SOME JOBS ARE ALWAYS DULL

What about jobs that are too difficult to change? You're not prepared to restructure the full-time receptionist's duties, the assembly line job, the quality inspector's duties, those of the letter sorter, or whatever the employee rates as boring. One option might be to share jobs among people. Let a few employees rotate jobs to split the monotony. Everyone can take a turn at mail sorting, or filing, or operating the switchboard.

But you may face the situation where the job simply can't be adjusted, enriched, enlarged or shared. And the job normally isn't boring. It's just that the person in the job has mastered it so quickly her performance now deteriorates with lack of stimulation. Essentially there's been an improper selection and although she has enormous capacity for more work, she is inappropriate for this specific job. If that's the case, bite the bullet, move her out and reassign her to a better-suited position. If that's not possible, dismissal may be the answer. But learn from this mistake and improve the selection criteria for the next time you fill the position.

---

### SUMMARY POINTS

- Boring jobs should be redesigned or restructured to reduce boredom, and to increase stimulation and intrinsic satisfaction for the employee.

- Build measurable short term goals into jobs so the employee can experience accomplishment and success.

- Try to match jobs with employee interest and aptitude levels.

# STEP 7

## I Can't Concentrate!

Are there job
distractions?

YES ────────────────▶ Remove
the dis-
tractions.

This particular problem is straightforward and so are the solutions. Sometimes people are distracted. Their attention wanders. Consequently, they simply don't do their jobs properly. The answer to the problem is to eliminate or reduce the distractions.

There are usually some obvious environmental distractions that can be dealt with easily: too much noise, bright lights, lights that aren't bright enough, windows, no windows, open windows and closed windows, too much heat or not enough heat. Any of these distractions can make it difficult for people to concentrate. Maybe there's too much activity going on and some people can't tolerate visual distractions. These are standard kinds of distractions.

But there are other types of distractions as well. There are social distractions, where people are continually distracted by friends, by people they work with, by the telephone, even by a need within themselves to interact with others. Some people have a need to be liked, so they're always doing things to increase the likelihood that others will want them around. That's a distraction, too.

It's important to remember that there are lots of job distractions and they come in all sizes and shapes. What's great for one person can irritate the beegeebees out of another. An entire group can be distracted by something or only one individual may be affected. The distraction may be a direct result of a physical or social distraction in the workplace or it may be due to an emotional upheaval in the employee's home life or social circle.

Other kinds of distractions include things psychological, like fear — fear for safety, fear of losing a job. Some people are so afraid they'll get hurt on the job that their minds wander. They are part of their own safety problem. Some people work in jobs where there are real hazards and they're distracted by concern for their health. Others are distracted by the fear of getting fired. An employee could be so afraid that she'll make a mistake and be dismissed that the thought becomes a self-fulfilling prophesy. Her fear takes her mind off her job and she makes the mistake she dreads.

## DISTRACTIONS ARE COMMONPLACE

A key thing to remember is that we all suffer from distractions. It's a natural thing for minds to wander sometimes. People can't concentrate 100 per cent of the time. Your job as manager is to minimize distractions on the job.

Consider a receptionist's job. It's standard for companies to want as much output from one clerical position as possible. Suppose a woman is hired as a typist and she doubles as receptionist as well. She's supposed to type while enduring innumerable distractions. She has to greet people and answer the phone. People walk by and talk to her and her attention is routinely disrupted. Yet she's expected to do all the typing accurately and quickly. Predictably problems arise.

Open area offices became popular a few years ago and they still dominate the general office layout. But despite the better ventilation and other advantages, for many this decor creates one big distraction.

Another distracting layout is encountered where the boss's desk is positioned up front, in the open, like a school teacher's desk, for unrestricted vision and hearing. When employee counselling or discipline is attempted, this "school marm" set-up is particularly distracting.

Where there are controllable job distractions, as in the cases above, remove them. If that's not possible, lower your expectations of the employee's performance.

SUMMARY POINTS
- There are many kinds of distractions: social, physical, psychological and emotional.
- Insure that the psychological and physical work surroundings help the employee do the job.

# HERMAN®

## "Can't you get on with your work without watching me all the time?"

# STEP 8

## Nobody Could Do All That!

| Is the job properly designed for the capacity of the average worker? | NO ———————————→ | Redesign or restructure the job, or let the employee delegate some of the duties. |

Maybe there's something wrong with the design of the job. Jobs ought to be designed so that the average person can do them. I'm not talking about unique jobs designed around one individual's special talents. I'm talking about most jobs.

By design of the job I mean the amount of work that has to be done by the employee who holds that position, the number of people the employee supervises, and how many different activities the job entails. As well, a job design includes how many places the person has to be in or go to, how many skills the person must have and how much knowledge is necessary to do the job.

What happens in many growing organizations is that jobs change. We throw on more activities because the person can continually handle more. Activities have been added over the years so that now it takes a superstar to fulfill the requirements of the job or someone who must be trained for five years. And still, good old steady Joe continues to cope with the increased work load and the increased responsibilities. When this happens, we sometimes miss seeing the breaking point until the employee finally reaches it. All of a sudden the job has more activities than even Joe can handle. What used to be a place of employment where people could pace themselves and do their work effectively has become a sweatshop.

## JOB DESIGNS CHANGE

In addition to jobs changing as organizations grow and expand, a job commonly changes to suit the person in that job. But what happens when, for example, the woman who used to work the front desk leaves? She'd been with her employer for twenty years and knew the place inside and out. She did all sorts of miscellaneous pieces of business, from replying to correspondence and ordering supplies to doing her work as an industrial accountant. Well, the multi-task job design just isn't appropriate for the average person anymore.

Likewise when good old Joe leaves and someone else comes in, we quickly find out just how closely the job was designed around the capabilities of that one person and he had developed the skills for doing all those tasks over a period of ten years. Now we ask someone new to come in and to perform at that level immediately. We fail to see it's virtually impossible. Instead of expecting the newcomer to perform with comparable expertise, take a fresh look at the job design. It might not be a feasible job.

## IS THE JOB DESIGN APPROPRIATE?

Whether or not you decide a job is designed properly depends on your performance expectations of a person in that position, on your own priorities, on the nature of the work and on the kind of department or company you're running. If you own your own company, be especially careful with job design. Owners often expect their employees to have the same motivation they themselves have. They may design jobs that are appropriate only for people with their same energy and commitment. As the owner, you don't mind doing all kinds of work, from preparing year-end financial reports to straightening up the lunch room. You have the company in your blood and a perspective of the whole operation. You know how all the different parts fit together. It's unrealistic though to expect a salaried employee who just wants a job to have the same commitment and motivation as you do.

# HERMAN®

## "You'll have to wait for your soup. I can't do everything!"

Changing a job is a hard thing to do, especially if someone is in it. That one job interrelates with many other jobs. If you begin to change the duties of one position, the change can have an impact on many other people in your company. So before you begin a massive restructuring approach, look at some simpler solutions. One option if the employee is in management, is to let her delegate some duties and authority to a subordinate. The restructuring could benefit several people in that it may increase the productivity and self-esteem of the whole department and decrease stress on the manager. That's a very handy way to change the job without having to cut any red tape or upset the bureaucracy.

Here's a situation where restructuring could be helpful. You have a manager working for you and he seems overworked. He's not coping with his job. It looks as if there's no way for that guy to handle forty subordinates and all his other job activities as well. But if you give this manager an opportunity to delegate some authority to subordinates (or teach him how) and thereby get rid of some of his mundane job duties, you may find that he can now handle the job.

Or, suppose your shop superintendent has inherited twenty new employees from an amalgamated division; there's no way she can handle the group successfully. Instead of splitting the group and hiring another person, ask her to delegate some of her simpler activities to a senior employee. This way, her job becomes a little easier and in the process you've given recognition to one of your potential supervisors.

---

### SUMMARY POINTS

- Make sure the work load of each job is sensible and not designed around the unique skills of the last incumbent.

- Delegation is an easy way to simplify a job without changing the formal job description.

# STEP 9

## Hey, I'm No Genius!

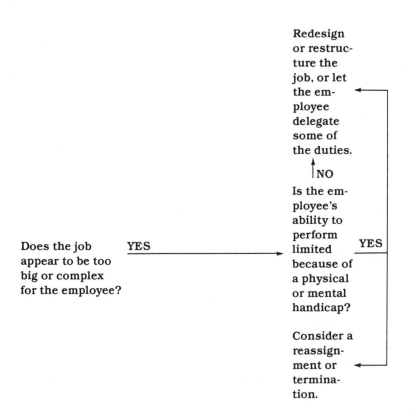

Does the job appear to be too big or complex for the employee? — **YES** → Is the employee's ability to perform limited because of a physical or mental handicap? — **YES**

**NO** ↑ Redesign or restructure the job, or let the employee delegate some of the duties.

Consider a reassignment or termination.

Let's say the job is reasonably designed. You know other people can do it, but it's just too big for this particular employee.

Some managers can easily supervise forty people. It's not impossible. Most draftspeople can produce their drawings on time and many nurses can handle a large number of patients. But if you decide that the job is too complex for a particular person, maybe you've made a mistake and put that person in a job he or she can't handle. That happens. Everyone makes selection errors.

We can't blame the employees for being selected by management to do a job they can't perform. The decision to hire them was wrong but it wasn't their fault. And what if they said they could handle the position? We can't blame them for trying to sell, or even oversell, themselves to get the job. The decision was management's, not theirs.

## IS THE EMPLOYEE'S ABILITY LIMITED?

If the answer is yes, and our subjective evaluation is that the job seems to be beyond this worker's capacity, we now ask, "Is this inability to perform due to a physical or a mental handicap?"

Suppose the employee can't do his job because of a physical disability. He might suffer from color blindness which hinders his work with electrical wires. Perhaps he has dyslexia, a visual problem that results in seeing words and letters switched around from the way they appear to others. Possibly his grasp isn't strong enough, he can't walk fast enough or he isn't mobile enough. Other possibilities are that he can't reach far enough, he can't react quickly, he's too short or too tall to do his job effectively. If his inability to do his job is a physical one, you might be able to redesign the job so that the inability doesn't affect performance.

Perhaps it's not really important, for example, that Peter, your warehouse supervisor, be the one to help unload deliveries. Maybe if John were scheduled to begin his shift fifteen minutes earlier he could do it. He's strong enough and he'd probably appreciate leaving earlier at the end of the day. Peter could then spend more time checking to see that all the inventory arrived.

Simple things like rearranging a person's desk, moving a book shelf or changing a working area to create space for a wheelchair can quickly take care of many performance problems stemming from particular physical inabilities.

Sometimes the performance problem can be due to a lack of intelligence, an inability to concentrate or some other type of cognitive problem. An example is not being able to grasp certain technical concepts necessary for the job. Or, possibly the job involves proofreading and the person has poor spelling skills. Poor reasoning abilities, undeveloped mathematical skills, limited abstract reasoning, poor conceptual skills and other similar problems could all be possible causes of performance problems.

At times the source of the problem may be emotional.

Maybe the new office manager doesn't have the emotional predisposition to develop good working relationships with the staff, and can only work alone.

Whether the handicap is physical, cognitive or emotional, there are two routes to go. The first is to restructure the job. You might find you can compensate for the incapacity with a new job design or by letting the employee delegate some of the job duties. By redesigning the job, you can help the employee become an effective member of your company. If this can't be done in a reasonable way, you may have to consider route two: reassigning the person to another job where the incapacity doesn't affect performance, or if that is not possible or desirable, terminating his or her employment.

## TERMINATION AS A LAST RESORT

When you are at the point where you're considering reassignment or termination, always look first to reassignment. You've already invested a lot of time and money in that employee: bringing the person in, making a selection and providing training for the job. Preserve that investment. Always look at alternatives before you consider firing.

One reason for reserving termination as the last resort is an ethical one. If people are in jobs they can't do, it's not their fault. It's your fault. You selected them or somebody selected them with management authority. Another reason is that it costs a lot of money to fire and replace somebody. In calculating the costs, the rule of thumb used to be one times the annual salary for that position. Now, for many jobs the factor has risen to 2.5 times the annual salary. If someone working for you earns $20,000, it will cost you from $20,000 to $50,000 to bring in somebody else plus cover expenses for recruitment, selection, placement and training. Preserve your investment and save additional expenses by trying to move these people into jobs they can do.

After all, it's an odd manager who junks a typewriter when it isn't working properly. If one part breaks down you wouldn't scrap it and buy a new one. However, don't get the idea you should retain an employee at any cost who is performing poorly. That's unfair to your other employees, to you and to your organization. Some employees will cost you much more if you keep them.

## LEARN FROM MISTAKES

There's an important lesson here for the manager. Try to avoid having this selection error happen again. Go back and review the data you used to make your selection decision in the first instance. What do you know now that you should have known then? What kinds of questions should you be asking when you interview future potential employees to ensure they are suited for the job? What can you be asking and measuring in the future so that you have the information you need to make good hiring decisions?

Theoretically, avoiding future selection errors should be an easy thing to do. We all resolve not to make such mistakes again. Simple as that. Surprisingly though the same mistake is made repeatedly in most organizations. When people fail in their jobs we just blame it on them. We say that they were no good. It would not occur to most of us that we were the ones who made the mistake. Instead our attitude is, "Let's try again and hope the next person works out better than the last." A better outlook would be, "We selected wrong. We must improve our selection techniques."

There's one final point to consider here. When the answer to the question about the employee's ability is, "No, the employee does *not* have a physical or mental incapacity," then we've come up against an inconsistency in our reasoning. We've said that the job ought to be done by anybody but it's too big for this employee; however in our judgement, this employee really doesn't have any limitations! In this case, it's possible we were wrong in our initial assessment that the job was properly designed and the algorithm tells us to reconsider redesigning the job or allow the employee to delegate duties.

---

### SUMMARY POINTS

- Check to see if the employee's poor performance is caused by management choosing the wrong person for the job. If so, find out why the decision was incorrect and learn from the error.

- Are the employee's physical, cognitive and emotional characteristics appropriate for the job? If they aren't, try restructuring the job or reassigning the employee to another job.

- Don't be too quick to fire. First try to preserve your investment in the employee.

# STEP 10

## But I Don't Know How!

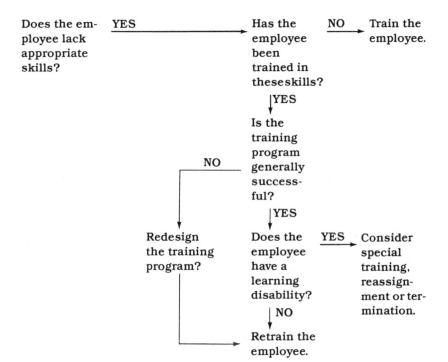

Does the employee lack appropriate skills? —YES→ Has the employee been trained in these skills? —NO→ Train the employee.

Has the employee been trained in these skills? ↓YES

Is the training program generally successful? —NO→ Redesign the training program?

Is the training program generally successful? ↓YES

Does the employee have a learning disability? —YES→ Consider special training, reassignment or termination.

Does the employee have a learning disability? ↓NO

Retrain the employee.

You've now looked at a number of causes for employee performance problems and it's still not clear why the employee can't do the job. Maybe your employee doesn't have the appropriate skills to do the job. This is not an uncommon problem. A great many employees are put in jobs without first receiving proper training.

If for some reason the employee lacks the skills, check to

see if she has ever been trained in those skills. If she hasn't been, then train her. There's a very old piece of wisdom that comes in handy for this question. Ask yourself: "If the employee's life depended on it, could she do the job?" If you believe the employee could do it with this ultimate motivation then she has the skills.

I'm not for a moment recommending that you threaten your employee to get an honest answer. But if it seems that there's no way the employee could do the job then you may have a skill problem on your hands.

## BE CAUTIOUS ABOUT
## ASSUMING A SKILL DEFICIENCY

Studies on employee ownership of companies have turned up some interesting points. In the past few years, many employee-owned companies have started up. It's surprising what happens when employees buy the shares in the company they work for. People start doing the job properly. Theft goes down. (Why steal from themselves?) Motivation increases and performance soars.

Sometimes it takes an emergency to help you discover whether or not performance problems are related to skill levels. Recently a manufacturing firm assumed its performance problems were mainly due to a lack of essential job skills. But when the company prepared to enter a trade show, the president sent a memo to all employees asking that display models be built perfectly. After all, these models would have to speak for the company's ability to deliver a good product. If the sample product looked really good, the company could expect a lot of business from this show. "Let's not make a mistake," the president beseeched, "these are our show pieces. Let's make them perfect." The employees responded by producing a perfect product. But if the employees can do that once or twice, why can't they do it again? The reason for past performance problems in this instance was not a lack of skill.

## INSUFFICIENT SKILL TRAINING
## A WIDESPREAD PROBLEM

Skill training in industry is deficient throughout North America. Very often it's this deficiency that's the real culprit for low productivity.

On one side of industry, there are the companies that excel.

They train their employees and they're proficient at it. They shine as examples to the rest of us. They produce good products efficiently and they deliver their services competently. Contributing immensely to their success is a serious commitment to skill training. They always teach their employees the skills needed to do jobs properly. If you look into any of the case studies on "excellent" companies, you'll find that this commitment to training is very strong. These companies have learned that high skill levels in production are very valuable assets.

On the other side of industry, there are many companies where teaching a skill amounts to this: "Watch Joe do it and pick it up from him." Bad habits are readily passed along while the good work habits fade away.

## USUALLY IT'S SINK OR SWIM

Consider this scenario:

> "Bill, you've been a ticket agent for our airlines for the past five years. You've done such a good job as an agent — perfect attendance, you are always punctual, your customer relations skills and knowledge of flight schedules are excellent — we want you to come in next week and be a pilot. So here are the keys to the 747 out back. Feel free to take it out for a spin. Now don't worry about the storm forecast for Monday. We have confidence in you and we'll be there all the way to back you up. Just put on your new uniform, hop into the plane and fly anywhere you want. Get a good feel for the plane and get to know the crew.
>
> "After a week or so, if you really think this job is going to suit you, we'll enroll you in a correspondence program offered through the local college. It's called "The Theoretical Foundations of Aviation." You take courses such as history of flight, aerodynamics and model airplane building. You also learn how to serve bar drinks and how to greet customers. It lasts for three years and at the end you get a certificate. Now, after those three years, if you've proven yourself a competent pilot and your performance appraisals are positive and, of course, you pass the certificate program, then we'll teach you how to fly the plane!"

Naturally, we would hope airline pilots aren't trained in this way. Yet this scenario closely corresponds to the sort of training managers receive in most organizations. People become managers precisely because they were so good at their non-management jobs. They were terrific so the boss promoted them. But the boss forgot to teach them how to manage. It's very odd to think that organizations would go ahead and hire people, pay them to do a job, yet not go that extra inch to teach them how to do the job. But they do. Instructions are: "Here's the job, you figure it out and if you succeed, we might put you on a course. But we won't teach you a thing beforehand. It's common sense."

That's not an extreme example. It's a common one. In some hospitals, for instance, it's common for nurses to be promoted to department head with next to no training. They are told one day, "You're the boss." The next day they come into a cluttered office and must figure out what they're supposed to do. We've surveyed many medical institutions to find out how much money they spend on training their managers. It's such a non-event in the industry that some have no idea what they spend.

Other industries omit training too. Think of all the excellent salespeople who were promoted to sales management and then were left alone to sink or swim. Most sink. Managers become executives but fail to learn new executive skills. Organizations create task forces, project teams, working committees and the like, but forget to teach the members how to develop groups, manage conflict or run meetings.

Lack of skills is a major cause of performance problems in all industries from the front-line managers to the executives. It isn't a so-called blue collar phenomenon. For business as a whole, over 90 per cent of the people responsible for managing have never received any formal training on how to do it. They just struggle along in their jobs, doing what is supposed to be obvious to someone with common sense. They learn as they go, make some whopping big mistakes along the way and unknowingly pick up many bad habits.

## EXAMINE YOUR TRAINING PROGRAMS

Maybe your employee has been trained but still isn't doing the job properly. When your answer to the second part of question ten is 'yes' (the employee has been trained but still isn't doing the job properly), your next question is this: "Is the particular training program generally successful?"

The woman you hired recently might have a masters' degree in business administration. Yet there are some management activities she can't handle and you seem to recall that the head of the sales department, a man you hired five years ago with the same background as this woman, had some trouble with these tasks as well. Ask yourself, "Is the MBA program giving graduates the expertise that my company needs? Is the program generally successful from our point of view?"

Employee training is an area in which a lot of organizations do not keep records. I suggest you should. Keep track of how much your employees benefit from training programs. You should keep records if you have your own in-house training programs or if you make use of external agencies, colleges, universities or private companies to do your training. Don't be shy about finding out if the people who take training programs come back with the skills that you want them to have. Don't presume that because somebody takes a course and gets a "certificate" that the course is effective and that it gives your employees what you expect. Just because somebody gets a degree in business administration from Ho-Dung Flats College doesn't mean he's learned what he's supposed to. Keep records for an objective assessment. Then, if your records indicate the training program is not generally successful, redesign it, send people somewhere else or hire people who were trained at some place other than Ho-Dung Flats.

In the case of a university or college program where you can't redesign the training program yourself, you can still recommend some changes. Take time to let the institution know the program's shortcomings. If the planners refuse to see the error of their ways, look around for other training programs. I've talked to company executives who complain about training programs they've sent people to and yet they continue sending their employees to the same program. Why? "Well, that's what we do. That's how we do things around here." Ridiculous! If the training program isn't successful, recommend that it be redesigned and retrain the employee or send the employee elsewhere.

You can correctly assume that no training program is perfect. For this reason, it makes good sense to keep track of what the program's strengths and weaknesses are so that it can be continually improved. Is it giving you what you want? Are your people usually coming out with the skills you expect them to have? Ask your employees before they go on a training course: "When it's over, what are you going to be able to do? How is that going to change how you do your job?" If your employees can't answer these questions, you're probably wasting money. And when a program is completed, your employees should show you what they can do. If they can't, don't send anyone again. Find another training program.

## IF THE PROBLEM ISN'T THE PROGRAM?

Suppose, though, that the training program is generally successful. Most people go through it and learn the necessary skills but your employee hasn't. Well, maybe your employee has a learning disability. He isn't picking up the skills because he's not able to learn as quickly as the average employee. Differences in rates of skill acquisition occur because people don't all learn at the same rate. If that's the case with your employee, why not consider special training? Could you restructure the training program and give the employee some special teaching aids to help with the learning process? The end objective is to have the employee learn the skills; it's not to get the person through the training program at the same speed as everyone else. I fail to see why we are intent on forcing everyone to learn at the same rate in the same manner and failing those who don't learn fast enough.

It's surprising how many formal training programs are based on the assumption that everyone learns at the same rate. For me, two subjects where this hits home are accounting and statistics. For both of these, the principles and procedures became clear to me at the end of the term and after a long, confusing struggle. After sweating away with the concepts, everything came together in the end. Put yourself in that position. What a shame if the light goes on in your head two days after the exam. It's too late; you fail the course. But if the light went on in your friend's head a day before the exam, your friend passes. So now your friend is an accountant and you're not, just because it took you a few days longer to get the hang of things.

There are other reasons why people may not do well with training courses. The training program you sent your welder to, for example, might rely heavily on written material. Your welder can't read very well. So the potentially perfect welder fails. Too bad he wasn't taught some other way.

One last point about training — if your employee doesn't have a learning disability but went through the training program without acquiring the skills taught, simply train the person again. There's no law that says you can only have one chance to learn. Certainly that's how some formal institutions operate.

But no one said you had to be antiquated in your company. "If you don't make it through this time," some institutions insist, "that's tough luck. We're not going to train you again." Some even think that this attitude is a symbol of high educational standards. More appropriately, it's a reflection of low teaching standards and intolerance for individual differences. It's a reflection on the people doing the teaching rather than on the people being taught.

## CONSIDER SPECIAL TRAINING

Final instructions under question ten, if there *is* a learning disability, are to consider special training, reassignment or termination. First of all, if someone working for you has a learning disability or lacks a secondary skill needed for a course, look to special training to compensate. Secondly, keep in mind that people learn at different rates when you retrain or reassign them. And look to these options before you plan to terminate employment.

Finally, don't jeopardize your investment in your employee. Don't discard the employee because your training approach didn't compensate for individual differences. Avoid forcing the "normal curve" on your employees, where the assumption made is that a certain percentage are always going to fail. Forget that. If you really want to capitalize on your human resource investment, compensate for individual differences and make it possible for everybody to pass.

---

### SUMMARY POINTS
- Employees who are placed in "sink or swim" situations usually sink.
- Make sure there really is a skill deficiency before prescribing training.
- Critically assess the success of all training programs. Don't assume they are well designed or appropriate.
- People all learn a little differently. Try to accommodate these differences.

---

# STEP 11

## Guess I'm Out Of Practice!

| | | |
|---|---|---|
| Does the employee lack skill practice? | YES ⟶ | Arrange for more skill practice. |

Sometimes people's skills get rusty. Because of a lack of use, some of the sharpness fades away and the person doesn't do as well as he should. Managers learn how to conduct performance appraisal interviews, for example, but appraisals are done infrequently, possibly only once a year, and so managers become awkward and ill-at-ease when giving appraisals. The solution is to practise the skill more often, perhaps in private or with another manager.

A management skill which often needs practice is disciplining. Suppose you learned how to discipline when you first became a manager. However you rarely used discipline. It's been two years since you were taught and only now do you have to implement disciplinary action. Instead of stumbling through the procedures, practise the discipline interview in advance. This also raises your self-confidence in performing the task and increases the likelihood you'll be successful.

Sometimes an employee just lacks a little practice in doing his job. Maybe it's a rare occasion when your painter has to paint the trim himself — his partner always used to do it. It would be reasonable to let him practise once in a while instead of chastising him for doing a poor job.

Perhaps there is an accounting or reporting procedure that is required very rarely, or a procedure a dental hygienist seldom uses, or a formula that is infrequently needed, and as a result the employee stumbles a bit and doesn't perform the task perfectly. These kinds of performance problem are the simpler ones to solve. All you have to do is make arrangements for practice. If you're not sure that practice is what's needed by your employee, ask the person to show you how to do the task in question. Then if it's not being done correctly and you know the employee used to be able to do it, the problem may be that he hasn't done it enough. Give him time and a place to practise and check back afterwards to find out if his skills have improved. Record the procedure for fast recall in the future. Don't depend on memory.

---

### SUMMARY POINTS
- Arrange for practice of infrequently used skills.
- Write down the procedure so no one forgets.

# STEP 12

## But There's Not Enough Time!

Does the employee perceive a lack of time? — YES → Reappraise the time frame for the assignment.

From research we know that one of the major factors influencing motivation is our expectation that we can actually do the job and be successful. That expectation of success is strongly influenced by our perception of resources available to us. Do we believe we have sufficient resources to get the job done?

Does your employee perceive a lack of time? Time is a critical resource. People are well aware that once it's spent it never comes back. So the employee's perception of whether there is sufficient time is a motivating (or demotivating) factor.

You cannot reasonably expect your employees to be "gung ho" to get the job done if they honestly believe there's not enough time. At times this perception can be a rationalization. People often have plenty of time to do an assignment yet still use lack of time as an excuse. And if they use the excuse often enough, they begin to believe it's true. Furthermore, if we think we don't have enough time to do the job, our tendency is to prove ourselves right. Consequently, we do whatever we can to make sure we don't get the job done on time. Our goal is to convince whoever needs to know that we were right; we didn't have enough time.

People who lack self-confidence are often guilty of using this crutch. So too are people who procrastinate. Lack of time provides a reason for not doing a job well. People sometimes procrastinate because they're insecure about their abilities. They're afraid they might fail. But if they procrastinate and as a result do fail, they can always say that they just didn't have enough time; that's why they failed. Hence, they can convince themselves that they're really "okay."

## "REAPPRAISE THE TIME FRAME"

On the other hand the employee may truly lack sufficient time to do the job well. Maybe you asked your salesperson to prepare a sales report every Saturday afternoon between sales calls. Well, it just so happens that that's the employee's busiest time with customers. Or you have asked the receptionist to type a report by noon, or the foreman to complete the product run by Friday. The employee may well perceive a lack of time to do the job.

Perception of time is key here. Set aside for a moment your judgement about whether there really is enough time. The important point is how the employee perceives time. If you do have an employee who believes he or she doesn't have enough time, then take another look.

Find out if the employee is right. You may have given her an assignment that you can do in that time frame, but she cannot. The employee is still learning the job and doesn't have your experience.

Suppose you have employees working on an assembly line. You believe they ought to be able to make ten widgets every five minutes. Your employees say, "No way. If you can do three of those you're doing very well." Yet you know it can be done and you want your employees to produce the items within this time constraint in order to meet performance standards. Or, suppose you're giving out assignments: "Here's a project I want you to do and I need it completed within a month." Or, "I want you to get next year's budget prepared in a week's time." Find out if these time constraints are reasonable. If they're not, lower your performance standards for the time being.

One often sees resistance in the workplace to attempts to speed things up. In factories, employees sometimes perform jobs at a slow pace and assume their way is the only way to do the job. With the new process, they perceive a lack of time. They may not realize the job can be done five times faster. They've never seen it done that fast before and they aren't familiar with the work pace. Their attitude is, "Show me. If you can't show me, I won't believe you."

Supervisors and managers frequently use "time" as the excuse for not supervising their employees better. "My day is full now. How can I do my job and all this supervisory stuff too?" Since Parkinson's Law is frequently true (work expands to fill the time available) there probably will be a time problem if work priorities aren't changed.

## KEY PROBLEM AREAS WITH TIME

Types of problems that arise due to time frames are completing projects on time and working at a particular pace. Make an effort to be fair in your assessment of time requirements. Your expectations may be totally unrealistic. You may have to negotiate agreeable terms with your employees.

If the time frame is rigid though, and the job must be done by a certain time, you're going to have to demonstrate that the job can in fact be completed. This will involve closer supervision. Work along with the employee providing a model of how the job is done at the pace or within the time you want. A practice some companies have adopted is to show videos of work activities to provide proof that the time is reasonable.

Think about how the employee perceives the time frame. Don't shorten someone's time frame believing that will help motivate him to work faster. That tactic can backfire and you'll end up with people working less, believing they can't get the job done on time.

---

### SUMMARY POINTS
- You can't motivate employees by setting unreasonable time limits.
- You may have to convince the employee that there is enough time.
- What counts is what the employee thinks.

# STEP 13

## There's No Way It Can Be Done!

Does the employee perceive a lack of tools, equipment, materials, funds, support staff or other resources? — YES → Reappraise the resource support including materials, funds, support staff, etc.

There are other resources besides time that people need to get the job done such as tools, equipment, materials, funds and budget, support staff and other job-related resources. Whether employees perceive these to be adequate will affect their expectation of success and hence their motivation.

Consider how your sales manager would react if you told her she'd have to increase sales by 50 per cent next year with no additional support staff and with last year's budget and print materials. Or maybe you have to tell your employees, "We've got to increase sales by 20 per cent and cut staff by 10 per cent." The groans begin. "Ah, there's no way we can do that."

Perhaps your employees must use equipment that is old and less efficient than the latest models. An employee moving to your division from another division of the company that had all the latest equipment will experience your division as sad by comparison. Although the equipment is functional, the employee says, "There's no way I can do my work with all of this old junk." The equipment works, sure, but it's not as sophisticated. The employee perceives this as a drawback. Whether it is or not, it's the employee's perception that will affect motivation.

A nurse transferring from a large metropolitan hospital to a small rural hospital is stymied. She doesn't know how people can ever give good health care in tiny, under-equipped places like this one. She misses the sophisticated equipment. Her perception of a severe lack of resources directly affects her motivation. She believes she just can't do her job without specialized equipment.

A plant superintendent is forever complaining, "I don't have the right staff working for me. How can I get the job done with the type of worker that Personnel keeps sending me?" And the advertising manager says, "I don't have enough money. We'll never make the proper media impact. Give me 30 per cent more and I can do something!"

## ONCE AGAIN, REAPPRAISE

Maybe the employee does face a shortfall in resources. If so, adjust your expectations accordingly. But if it's simply a feeling the person has that she can't do it, tighten supervision. You must show your employees that they can manage within those limited resources.

If you were the sales manager charged with increasing sales by 20 per cent while cutting staff by 10 per cent, you could face an immediate drop in employee morale. To prevent this from happening, step in immediately and work directly with your staff. Set out action plans. Ask your employees how they're going to accomplish this. Understand their problems, but be firm about the new standards. Let them know the job can be done. Set up a reporting schedule to be sure they're on track. Keep your employees motivated by working at bolstering confidence and letting them know you appreciate their co-operation and efforts.

If resources are in short supply, level with the employees. Tell them that's the way it's got to be this year. Let your employees know that you're aware of what they're up against. Ask them for their co-operation and recognize their achievements.

Don't attempt to motivate people by withholding supplies or resources. It won't make them try harder to achieve. There are a few people, of course, who might surprise you with a positive response to withheld resources and lack of time. A few might try harder just to prove they can rise to all occasions despite the obstacles but for most people motivation will drop drastically. Employees are more likely to say, "Why should I try? They don't give you the resources around here to get the job done." As a result they don't try as hard and a self-fulfilling prophecy begins.

---

**SUMMARY POINTS**

- Believing that the job can't be done because of a lack of resources usually becomes a self-fulfilling prophesy.

- Be reasonable in your expectations.

- Be prepared to sell the idea that there are sufficient resources to get the job done.

---

# STEP 14

## But You Said It Was O.K.!

| Is the employee's poor work being rewarded? | YES ─────────────────▶ | Eliminate the inappropriate reinforcers and reinforce the good behaviors. |

It sounds strange, but an employee's poor work is often rewarded. "But why," you say, "would a boss ever reward poor work? That's rather dense." Surprisingly, it's a common occurrence. Take, for example, the employee who sloughs along, doesn't really work hard and doesn't get the job done. What happens? The boss steps in and takes work away from him, saying, "Oh well, he can't really handle that. I'd better give him easier jobs." Subtly, the employee's poor work is rewarded — he gets fewer assignments and those he gets are the easiest ones.

Alternatively, it might not be the boss who's rewarding poor work. Many of the rewards that an employee gets can be ones that we're not aware of or that we have no control over. That is, nobody is running up to the employee and thanking him for poor work. But interpersonal relations and the procedures of the organization sometimes end up functioning as a reward for the employee.

Consider the typist who does poor work. As a result of the poor quality, we take work away from her. We don't want to give her any more work because she may mess it up. She learns that if you take your time and make lots of mistakes, everyone will pitch in and help you.

The man who perpetually comes to meetings late by five or ten minutes always gets a fuss made over his lateness. Intrinsically, that could be rewarding for him. He might like all that attention. Meanwhile, we're wondering why he keeps coming in late.

Sometimes companies reward poor work with a promotion. It happens that departments get rid of poor workers by promoting them to other areas of the company. "Let's get rid of old Fred. Let him be a bother somewhere else. We'll tell the other department that he's really good." We counsel the person into the other job. Away Fred goes, rewarded for his poor work.

In the retail trade, sometimes a manager comes in and plays around with the inventory, either building up or depleting stock for the period she's there. By doing so she inflates the profit picture to look as if the department has really done well. She then walks away with a promotion. Or you get a boss with a cruel, authoritarian and manipulative management style literally whipping people into submission to get work done. In the short run, the boss gets high production out of the department and gets a promotion because of that performance. Meanwhile, the seeds of absolute disaster have been planted. The next manager steps in and the place is a mess. Meanwhile, the first manager who got the promotion ended up having his short-term management style reinforced. The higher-ups have said, "You're a good manager. We like your results." The manager learns that people can be jumped on and you can work the living daylights out of your staff. That's what the brass want. Short-term poor work has short-term positive spin-offs and brings rewards.

Here are a few other examples of poor work being rewarded. The less time someone spends with customers, the more likely it is the person can take a longer coffee break. In fast food service, the employee is rewarded for the number of orders rung through the till, but to increase numbers may mean giving discourteous service. In the short run employees are rewarded for increased customer volume but indirectly they are rewarded for giving poor customer service.

The solution to these problems is to eliminate inappropriate reinforcers and to reinforce the good behaviors.

## THE CONCEPT OF REINFORCERS

The concept of reinforcers comes from the reinforcement theory of motivation. Under this theory, the consequences the employees experience as a result of performance are a determining factor in future performance. If good consequences follow the work, employees are inclined to do that work; if undesirable consequences follow their work, they are less likely to do that work.

Reinforcers, the good consequences of behavior, come in all shapes and sizes. There are social reinforcers and monetary ones. There are extrinsic rewards from sources outside the person such as gifts or praise and there are intrinsic rewards, the things people feel within themselves such as a sense of pride, achievement or joy. It's difficult to be aware of these intrinsic rewards yet they are important determinants of how people perform their jobs.

Technically speaking there are two types of reinforcement — positive and negative. Positive reinforcement occurs when, as a consequence of your action(s), you receive something you like and as a result you tend to repeat the action(s). For example, you do something and for it receive a gift. If you like the gift you're prone to repeat whatever you did that resulted in receiving the gift.

Negative reinforcement occurs when something that you don't like is taken away from you as a result of some action of yours. For example, when work which we don't like to do is taken from us, we feel better.

Often, negative and positive reinforcement go hand in hand. Suppose you are visiting neighbors and their three-year-old keeps hitting you on the shin with a heavy toy. You'd like to get rid of the little pest so you try to ignore him. That doesn't work. He just hits harder. You reach into your pocket and, thank goodness, you find some candies. You give some to the child and say, "Be a good boy and go and play somewhere else!" The little boy leaves and you figure you've solved the problem.

But have you? The boy has been hitting your shin and as a result he gets a candy. You have positively reinforced his behavior with that candy. Next time he wants candy or attention, your shin is really in for it. And what has happened to you? You gave him candy and as a consequence he disappeared. Your act of giving candy was negatively reinforced by his leaving. The next time he pesters you, you're likely to give him candy again to get rid of him. Instead of solving the problem, you've increased the likelihood it will happen again.

Or how about this scenario. Harold, your bookkeeper, is always complaining about walking two blocks to the post office to register mail. That's part of his job, but he hates to move a muscle and would sooner sit and total columns. His complaining is so aggravating, you ask Frieda to take the mail. But what has Harold learned? Complain enough and the boss will get someone else to do it. Giving in to chronic complainers just reinforces the complaining.

## GET RID OF INAPPROPRIATE REINFORCERS

You have to ask yourself, "If the person is acting inappropriately, is it because the action is reinforced or encouraged?" Jack fools around in the fibreglass spray booth. Is he being rewarded for that behavior? Maybe everybody laughs. Jack gets attention and he loves it. His behavior will continue as long as the reinforcement is there.

An employee is continually handing in reports late and full of errors. What happens? Someone else takes over the job, makes the corrections and finishes it off quickly. Or we take the workload away from the person. "She's going to get that in late; we had better give her less to do next month." Her tardiness will continue until we say, "Hold it." We can't reward people for getting work in late. There has to be some price to pay, some unpleasant consequence.

While you're weeding out reinforcers of poor behavior, try to reinforce the good behavior. Going back to Jack's antics in the spray booth, monitor his behavior more closely. When you see occasions where he went through a whole day without horsing around, reward his behavior in some meaningful way. Try appealing to his mature side, taking him aside and thanking him. Or give him attention for something you approve of. You may be able to set up an occasion where Jack does something well and the other employees give social approval. Another strategy is to allow him to satisfy his clowning instincts at some other place and time.

Watch to see if poor work is being reinforced or encouraged by some external force. But be prepared — you may be that external force. Many times your behavior as the manager is perceived by your employees to be a consequence of their behavior. Your actions, words and behavior may follow what the employee has just said or done in such a way that you encourage or discourage something without being aware of it.

## DON'T LOOK THE OTHER WAY

Suppose there is a rule that people must follow and they know there is a penalty for not following it. If they don't follow the rule but they aren't penalized, the boss has indirectly rewarded them for not following the rule since they see that they have avoided the deserved penalty. Avoidance of something unpleasant that is deserved is a form of reward.

While driving on the highway who ever goes the speed limit? Most people go a little faster if they can. When you see a police car up ahead, you see potential punishment and you slow down. You drive within the limit with one eye on the police and one on your speedometer. But once the potential for punishment becomes remote, away you speed. Society directs the police to use punishment to control behavior, but it's a very weak way to enforce behavior. It backfires when you speed but don't get a ticket, telling you that tomorrow if you speed the chances are good you won't get a ticket then either. You've avoided the punishment you know you should have received. When that fear of punishment is taken away from you (an example of negative reinforcement), you're encouraged to speed the next day because you didn't get caught the first day. And because everybody can't get caught all the time — there simply aren't enough police officers around — one could argue that ticketing speeders may only encourage speeding. If you do get caught, you say, "Tough luck. I got dinged today. My luck was bad." But the odds are good you won't get caught again for a while. Back come the old habits.

What would happen if instead of being punished for speeding you were rewarded for driving within the speed limit? Police could randomly pull people over. "We monitored you for the last five kilometers and you were going within the limit. That's really good. We're going to give you a reward." Your insurance premium could be reduced. The police could hand you ten dollars or an award citation. If you thought today might be the day you would be rewarded for driving properly, the likelihood of you driving within the speed limit would be increased.

Many cities have "safe driving" weeks. For one week during the year, the police actually pull people over to give them a citation for their good driving habits. During safe driving weeks, the common finding is that people do drive more safely and they don't speed as much. So there is a strong case for rewarding people for their good behavior rather than always trying to catch them doing something wrong.

**SUMMARY POINTS**
- Don't inadvertently encourage poor work or inappropriate behavior.
- Your behavior is frequently perceived by your employees to be a consequence of their behavior.
- Reinforce appropriate behavior.
- Be aware of what employees regard as rewards and recognition.
- Be aware of what happens to your employees immediately after they do some inappropriate work.
- If rules are to be followed, you must enforce them consistently.

# STEP 15

## Thanks For Nothing!

| | | |
|---|---|---|
| Is the employee's | YES | Eliminate |
| good work being | ———————→ | the sources |
| punished? Is | | of punish- |
| there peer pres- | | ment and |
| sure against | | reinforce |
| good work? | | the good |
| | | behaviors. |

It's possible that people don't do good work because whenever they do they are punished. But why would the boss punish someone for doing good work? What on earth for? Well, it does happen.

Here's a classic example. You have a staff of ten people. Two of them are excellent workers. They do any job quickly and accurately. You also have a few people who seem hopeless. They do poor work in twice the time it takes the good workers. Suddenly, you have extra work coming in which can land you a new contract. It has to be done right away and it's got to be done accurately. So whom do you go to to get the job done — your best workers or your poor workers? What do most of us do? We don't give the job to our poor workers, you can be sure, because they'd do a terrible job and they might not finish on time in which case we would not get the contract. We give the assignment to our best workers. It's obvious. What else could we do?

The trouble is, you do that too often and the good workers feel as if they're being dumped on. Whenever there's extra work to do, we go to them. However, we're taking the risk they'll perceive that their good work is being punished. In other words, "The harder you work around here, the more the boss dumps on you." Hard-working employees soon become scarce and everybody tries to become invisible.

Take the case of the employee who scrimps and saves to underspend her yearly budget by 10 per cent. After saving her company a lot of money, her department promptly gets 10 per cent chopped off next year's allotment. That's the last time she'll ever underspend a budget. In fact, in the last month of a fiscal year she'll probably spend vigorously to use up any surplus.

Have you ever been asked by the boss to think up lots of ideas to promote the business, but then you were shot down in flames because the ideas weren't good enough, or they were termed stupid, naive, or ill-conceived? Well maybe some were, but that's the last time you'll give any ideas to the boss.

Although it isn't our intention to punish good employees, intention here doesn't count. What counts is how our actions or words are perceived.

## MANAGERS WHO THANK EMPLOYEES FOR POOR WORK AND PUNISH THEM FOR GOOD WORK ARE RARE, RIGHT?

No. Many managers inadvertently do just that. The results are low morale and poor performance. In the example where extra work surges into a department, the appropriate thing to do is share the workload. Make sure your poor workers don't remain poor workers. Make them do their share. You may be faced with a dilemma, of course. "The work has to get done and I can't give it to John and Jane. Just this once, I'll give it to my good workers." Recognize that eventually you have to start managing this department effectively. You have to improve the performance of the poor workers to an acceptable level while recognizing, "If I *must* give more work to my good workers now, then I'll have to reward them for performing beyond the levels of the other workers."

There has to be something in it for them. The kind of reward depends on the particular job and each situation. Perhaps it's a bonus, time off, praise or recognition. Sometimes praise is given so infrequently that just a bit works wonders, such as a thank you for the extra work or some attention from the boss. Or you could jot down some notes in the employee's file and take these comments into account when awarding raises next time around. Whatever your approach is, let the employee see that there is in fact a reward for good work.

There are many instances where rewarding poor work occurs simultaneously with punishing good work. You have a group of people working for you and one or two of them do poor work. You are forever working closely with them — supervising, coaching, encouraging. Unknown to you, that's exactly what they want. They like to get the boss's attention. Meanwhile your good workers in the department feel they have just as much right to your attention but they don't get it. You're too busy spending all your time with the poor workers. The others work hard yet they don't get any recognition from the boss.

Somehow you must learn to divide your attention equitably among your staff yet still get the poor performers on track. Using a performance profile (from Step 2) might help in recognizing good performance without using valuable time.

## PEER PRESSURE ENTERS IN

Is there peer pressure against good work in the group you manage? That happens. Co-workers use peer pressure, called "pinging", by cajoling and joking and cracking not-so-funny jokes. They pressure the good workers by saying things like, "Why are you working so hard? Pace yourself. Why do you suck up to the boss?" This is an adult version of the teacher's pet syndrome.

People are often discouraged through social pressure from doing good work. Many managers are inclined to believe that peer pressure doesn't exist or that their employees are so terrific they can rise above it. I think you're asking a lot when you ask an employee to rise above peer pressure.

Peer pressure is a fact of life. And when there's pressure against good work, you have to ask yourself, "Why is it taking place in my department? My school? My company? Why are my employees trying to discourage others from doing good work? Are they jealous? Do they feel that they never get recognition for their good work? Do they think someone else will receive all the recognition? What's the reason?" If people are discouraging good work you know there's something wrong. You could be the cause of it or it could have been caused over the years by an organization that never seemed to care or reward its employees for their efforts. They've become frustrated. Maybe they believe, "If you work hard around here you don't get ahead anyway."

---

### SUMMARY POINTS

- Be aware of good employee performance and give it recognition.
- Don't inadvertently discourage or shrug off any good work or behavior of your employees.
- If the work group discourages good performance by employees, find out why.

---

# STEP 16

## Nobody Tells Me Anything!

| Is the employee's good work being extinguished? | YES →————————→ | Start an appropriate reinforcement schedule for the employee's good behaviors. |

Extinction happens when there is no consequence to good behavior. Somebody does good work and nothing good happens. Likewise nothing bad happens. There are no encouragements, no discouragements. There's "nothing in it" for the person to do good work because it results in nothing. If this takes place often enough, the behavior will disappear. Sometimes, it can disappear quickly, or the pattern can be a slow fade.

Think of the new employee who comes to work on time every day for the first few months. Soon the employee sees that nobody else makes it to work on time. All the other employees drift in as they like. And the boss doesn't say to the new employee who is punctual, "Thank you, we appreciate your coming to work on time." After a while the employee thinks, "Why should I bother? Nobody else really struggles. I guess it isn't that important around here."

He starts to slip up and he comes in late like everybody else. There are no penalties, although the boss does start muttering a bit. Eventually, the new employee thinks to himself, "I'm one of the gang now. I feel as if I'm a full-fledged member of this company. I'm like everybody else with all the rights and privileges to break rules." When this happens, it is not the employee's fault. It's the manager's fault for not having reinforced the employee for being on time. The manager has not shown why it is important, nor has he shown that it is observed and appreciated.

Even if you're in a two-person office, extinction of a good behavior can still happen. If your partner is now coming in late whereas she always used to come to work on time, maybe she can't see any rationale for bothering any more. You never said it was important.

## GOOD WORK JUST FADES AWAY

Suppose you work late into the night every day for a month to handle a special assignment the boss gave you. You sweat and struggle to complete it on time. Two weeks after you hand it in the boss still hasn't acknowledged that she even received the report. You approach her and ask if she was satisfied with it. "Oh sure," she says. "Yes, it was quite good." What are the chances you'd work as hard the next time? Your efficiency would soon diminish under this boss.

Because good behavior can unwittingly be extinguished, it's critical that performance feedback be given throughout the year and not just at the year-end performance appraisal interview. Managers should also make sure that this continual performance feedback includes good work as well as bad. Don't assume your employee knows you are aware that he is doing good work or that he even knows that his work is good. He might not know it so it should be drawn to his attention. He should know on an ongoing basis that he is doing good work and that the work is appreciated.

Never presume that a paycheque will serve as a reinforcement. A pay system for the most part is an unsuccessful motivator and can't be used as a reinforcer. It's not because money can't motivate. Money does. But a paycheque is an administrative procedure. You get paid every two weeks because two weeks have gone by and you weren't fired. You don't receive your paycheque because of all the little things that you've done well in the past two weeks. It's because the earth has gone a little farther around the sun and it's time to issue cheques. And so the paycheque is rarely seen as a consequence of good work.

It would be silly, then, to assume that people will know they're doing good work simply because they get their scheduled paycheque. There has to be some other feedback, preferably verbal and possibly documented. Otherwise, good behavior disappears. And that's exactly what happens if your style is to say to the employee, "Unless you're getting heck, you know you're doing good work." The good work just fades away.

## AVOID EXTINGUISHING GOOD BEHAVIOR

Managers need to start appropriate reinforcement schedules for their employees. Start to be aware of good work. And by good work, I mean the specific behaviors that people perform competently in their jobs, not just the spectacular performances. So first of all, you the boss have to be aware of the employee's good behavior and then you have to start to reinforce that behavior. Usually all you will need is the verbal reinforcement. "I noticed what you did. It was important for this reason. Thank you." You could also document the behavior in the employee's file, which the person should have access to.

The term "reinforcement schedule" means the frequency with which you reinforce someone. There are no magic guidelines to follow. Once in a blue moon may be fine. You don't have to be thanking people all the time. There's no need to say, "Thanks for coming to work today, and I was very glad to see that you arrived promptly on time for the nineteenth time this month. When I spoke to you about your timeliness yesterday I forgot to thank you for coming to work and being on time on Monday as well." It isn't necessary. Just once in a while is fine. It all depends on what behaviors you're trying to reinforce. For things like perfect attendance and getting to work on time, once or twice a year is probably enough — especially if the behavior is documented on paper. The employees can see for themselves that, "Hey, this boss is aware."

## WHEN YOU MANAGE PEOPLE
## YOU MANAGE THEIR BEHAVIOR

Your function as a manager is to influence the behavior of people under you so that they do their jobs at the performance standards that you require. It's your job as well to discourage them from doing things that are harmful to the functioning of the work group. To achieve these ends, you have to be aware of their behavior. You can then perpetuate good behavior by encouraging it. Finally, do whatever you can to eliminate or decrease the poor behavior. Do that by discouraging it, not encouraging it.

---

### SUMMARY POINTS
- Don't let your employees labor in obscurity.
- Give recognition for consistent good work and not just for the spectacular.
- Don't assume employees know you appreciate their work.

---

# STEP 17

## I Don't Understand!

Did the employee misunderstand directions? —— YES ——→ Does the employee have a learning disability?

|NO → Re-explain directions and ensure two-way communication.

|YES → Compensate for learning disability or consider a reassignment or termination.

Sometimes employees simply misunderstand directions. Their hearts are in the right place, they sincerely want to do the job properly, but they did not understand what was required. For example, you ask Jim to make a thousand copies of a report. He misunderstands you and makes a thousand copies of a part of the report. Or he thought in total it was to be a thousand pages. The report was ten pages so he made you a hundred copies. There's always ample opportunity for people to misunderstand directions.

Or you instructed Janet to "think about" how you could redesign the plant layout, and she spent $15,000 for a consultant to reorganize the factory!

If you find that your employee did misunderstand directions, then you should ask yourself, "Does the person have a learning disability?" If mistakes happen often due to misunderstandings, it's possible the person has a problem understanding. And it doesn't just have to be understanding verbal instructions that is involved. The instructions could have been written and the employee read them wrong.

There are many kinds of learning disabilities. A high proportion of North Americans can't read adequately. They don't understand terminologies and so they misunderstand directions.

It could be an intelligence problem. The person doesn't have the reasoning ability for the type of job he or she holds. It's not uncommon for people to have very good skills for getting jobs. They know how to be interviewed and they know how to get the job but they simply don't have the intelligence to do the work. They can't learn quickly enough.

If a learning disability is causing the problem, compensate for it if you can. Maybe the person can't understand written instructions very well but can readily absorb verbal instructions. Then give instructions verbally as well and the problem is solved. Maybe the employee, a poor reader, read in a manual how to do a task and misunderstood the instructions. If we could show her a picture or a film of how to do it, we've taken care of the problem. Although compensating for individual differences takes some effort on your part, the expense and the time it takes to offer alternatives are usually worthwhile.

Better eyeglasses or a hearing aid might do away with "misunderstanding" immediately. If there's a language problem where an employee doesn't understand the working language of the shop floor, get someone who can translate. Try to compensate for the disability.

If you can't compensate for the disability and the employee simply cannot understand your directions then you're going to have to reassign that person to a job that he or she can do. Alternatively you may have to let the person go.

However, if the employee doesn't have a learning disability and yet he misunderstands directions, then try re-explaining the directions.

## GIVE INSTRUCTIONS AGAIN — WITH FEEDBACK

This time, ensure two-way communication. It's extremely important. As a general rule of thumb, if an employee misunderstands directions from the boss, it's never the employee's fault. It's always the boss's fault. Always. It is the responsibility of the

# HERMAN®

"Sorry!"

person who sends information to make sure that the other person understands what was sent, especially if there is a status or power difference between the two such as boss and employee.

It's always the boss's fault. Even if the employee says, "Yes, I understand," and the boss says, "Are you sure you do? I don't want you to leave this office until you clearly understand," and the employee says, "I absolutely understand fully and completely, really I do," and then goes ahead merrily making mistakes. Maybe the employee did understand, absolutely, perfectly — to the employee's understanding but it wasn't the same understanding the boss had. You can't fault employees for conscientiously believing they knew what the boss wanted done.

Two-way communication means the boss has to make sure there's some feedback to show that the employee absorbed what the boss communicated. The boss has to say something like, "Okay, put into your own words what I just asked you to do. I want to see if I was clear." Or have your subordinates write a memo to you showing in their own words their comprehension of your instructions. Never accept a "yes" as proof that the employee understood. And never say, "I'm going to tell you once and if you don't understand, it's your fault." Eventually, it's going to fall back on your lap. If you have to tell your employee ten times, tell him ten times. It'll give you practice learning how to say it better. And practice you'll need, because in the end the responsibility for communication always rests with you.

---

## SUMMARY POINTS
- Recognize and compensate for an employee's learning or comprehension difficulty.
- If your employee misunderstands you, it's your fault.
- Real communication has to be two-way. Insure that there is feedback.

# STEP 18

## Guess I Forgot!

| Did the employee forget to do the job? | YES ⟶ | Act according to the seriousness of the issue. Try a mechanical solution. |
|---|---|---|

People aren't perfect and at times they simply forget. It's unrealistic to assume that people in your organization will do everything correctly all the time, never making mistakes and never forgetting things.

"I forgot," isn't necessarily the lame excuse it appears to be. The employee could have forgotten to do some part of the job. Maybe she forgot to lock up the office, to turn off a machine, to put supplies away or to finish a task because she got sidetracked and lost sight of the goal. Many things can be forgotten, some minor, some major.

## AN OUNCE OF PREVENTION

To help jog your employees' memories there may be mechanical procedures that can be employed such as rearranging the layout and mechanical operations associated with a task to ensure that important procedures are followed. For instance, your employees may have to wear protective safety goggles whenever they operate equipment. To help them remember, instruct your employees to hang their safety goggles on the equipment rather than a nearby hook whenever the goggles are taken off. In fact, take that hook away. They're to use the receptacle you set up on the machine itself. This way, the employees can't use the equipment until the safety goggles have been removed. A little reminder is sitting there right in front of the employee: "Hey, I'm supposed to put these things on."

How often do managers complain when the secretary forgets to avoid using white-out. "Look at this mess. Why can't she remember that I don't like white-out guck on my letters?" As a simple solution, don't buy the white-out. Throw it out. Now she can't forget and accidentally fall back to using it.

Check-lists are a big help when it comes to forgetfulness. You might write a list of steps to follow when starting up or shutting down a machine. Then post the list on the machine. Do what you can to help people remember to do things, in the order they're supposed to do them. If employees forget to turn off the lights, use signs that say, "Turn off the lights." Install mechanical buzzers to indicate that the lights have to be switched on or off. Buzzers used for seatbelts, in-car lights and car keys have proven to be useful for reminding people to do certain things at particular times.

## CAN IT BE FORGIVEN?

When employees do forget, act according to the seriousness of the issue. An error of omission which causes a minor problem is best excused. If, on the other hand, someone forgets to do a task and the error practically bankrupts your company you will have to make a judgement call, an ethical decision about keeping the person in your employ. If the task was such an important one though, and because of an employee's loss of memory the company was severely hurt, then the proper protection systems weren't in place to begin with.

If a stockbroker forgets to sell your stock at a particular time, she has to face certain consequences. She may lose your account. She could suffer some penalty with her own company and get raked over the coals by her boss. People are going to be angry. But for that one instance, she probably shouldn't be fired. However, if a pattern establishes itself or a second serious mistake is made, then yes, that person could be fired. The company just can't cope with such oversights — especially if no one else but this person forgets. Maybe someone forgets to lock the office and the office gets robbed. Well once, it can happen. Twice?

Three times? Your response may rightly be, "I'm sorry, we just can't tolerate that."

What you have to do as the employer is try whatever you can to make sure it doesn't happen in the first place. Try to build reminders into the job. If reminders don't work and people still keep forgetting, the problem may be a lack of attention. Or possibly the person isn't taking the job seriously. Depending on the seriousness of the error and how often it takes place, your response could range from a mild reprimand to major discipline or termination.

---

**SUMMARY POINTS**
- Anticipate that people do forget.
- Prevent "forgetting" with a technological or mechanical solution.

---

# STEP 19

## So Who's Perfect?

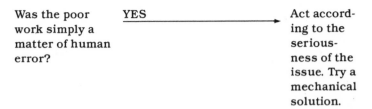

| Was the poor work simply a matter of human error? | YES ──────────▶ | Act according to the seriousness of the issue. Try a mechanical solution. |

It isn't that someone forgot to do the job or didn't understand what was to be done. He just made a mistake.

## ERRORS CAN BE AVOIDED

When we design machinery, we take into account an error factor. The factor may be a minor one but we know there will be errors. Machines don't work perfectly all the time. For this reason, we plan maintenance schedules and other means of checking our systems. We anticipate that things will go wrong and do whatever we can to minimize possibilities for error.

Likewise with people, we must assume that they too will make mistakes now and then. When employees learn new skills, they're bound to make some errors. A loss of attention from monotony on the job, distractions from things they're thinking about or inability to concentrate for an extended period of time will also generate errors. Someone will calculate wrong. Somebody will make a judgement error. There are methods though by which we can reduce the possibility of error in our systems.

If you produce printed material, have some system in place to enforce proofreading in order to catch mistakes before your product leaves the shop. Have the typesetter initial the back of the typeset page to show that the work was proofread. Whenever the boss sees those initials, she will know the piece has been checked and is supposed to be free of errors. If your company handles huge amounts of cash and your staff makes evening deposits to the bank, devise a plan to reduce the chances of error. It may be that your cashiers make more mistakes counting money as the evening wears on. In this case set up a system to minimize mistakes and schedule the employee breaks so that cashiers don't become exhausted. Look for ways to help your cashiers tally their evening deposits. Maybe they need a room to themselves while they're counting. Call for early deposits and have your assistant manager double count all cashier deposits before you do the final count. Simple procedures like these can help minimize the possibility of error.

Accept that mistakes will still happen now and then and when they do, act according to the seriousness of the issue. How often employees make mistakes is another thing. Maybe there's some sloppiness to be dealt with or lack of skill. Perhaps poor work is being reinforced or it has been in the past.

It could be that your performance standards aren't realistic, that they call for perfection. That's an admirable goal, but if employees are reprimanded because they're not always doing everything perfectly then they're working for an unrealistic boss.

---

### SUMMARY POINTS
- Anticipate mistakes and design systems and procedures to catch errors.
- Set realistic performance standards for your employees. Don't expect perfection.

# STEP 20

## Hey, I've Got Other Problems Too!

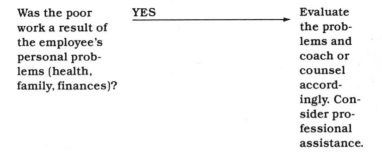

It would be convenient if employees left all of their problems at home. But they don't.

Family troubles, financial worries, physical and mental stress, social problems, or alcohol and drug abuse may overwhelm an employee and affect performance at work. Detecting the onset of a problem isn't always easy but dealing with it in its early stages can help prevent more serious problems developing.

### WATCH FOR SYMPTOMS OF THE PROBLEM

Sudden changes in personality can indicate health problems. People's personalities and their patterns of behavior are generally quite stable. They don't suddenly change without reason. So if you witness a surprising change in your employee's behavior, it could be a warning sign that something is wrong physically or mentally, or a new drug may be causing unwanted side effects. For financial problems, you might hear via the grapevine that one of your employees is having difficulties, or the employee may tell you personally. You may even know your people well enough to recognize when something is wrong.

## WHAT DO YOU DO NEXT?

The first rule of thumb is this: never set yourself up as an expert in a field in which you're not legally qualified. No one should ever do that. But particularly because you are "the boss," you must not give counsel as though you were an expert. Don't give medical counselling, financial counselling, marital counselling or any other kind of counsel or advice in an area in which you aren't licensed. You are setting yourself up to be sued.

Suppose you advise an employee on how to resolve a marital problem or how to take care of a financial problem. "Why don't you sell off those bonds, Mary," you say to her one day, "and put your money into stocks." The employee does it. She loses her shirt as a result of it. Or, "I've been thinking about you and Bob and I think that this is how you could take care of your marital problems." And then the marriage falls apart. She loses all her money, she loses her husband and her health deteriorates.

You may be wide open to being summarily sued by that employee. Of course, you didn't say you were an expert. In fact, you clearly recall telling Mary, "Look, I'm no expert in these matters. But if I were you..." You have to remember that you are in a position of authority. There is some obligation on the part of the employee, whether actual or psychological, to do as the boss says. Why? Because you're the boss.

Instead of offering advice, help the employee recognize how the problem is hurting him on the job and why he should do something about it. Then steer him in the right direction so that he can get professional help for his health problem or financial problem or whatever. Many companies have an employee assistance program for this purpose. Even small companies on modest budgets can afford the effort it takes to help their employees contact the appropriate social agencies.

If the employee has a drinking problem or a drug problem, you should get in touch with the counselling service first before approaching him. Ask the agency what you should do. Through their experience in dealing with these problems, they'll be able to offer good suggestions. What should you say to an employee in such cases? Should you say anything? They'll advise you of the best approach to take.

You can't force an employee to seek help nor can you "cure" the person. But then, your role is not that of a social agency so don't be too discouraged if the employee does not respond to your attempts to help him.

## YOUR ROLE IS TO BE THE BOSS

Your obligation as boss is to point out job behaviors that are inappropriate. Let it be known to the employee that poor performance will not be tolerated. "You can't come to work smelling of alcohol, you can't sleep on the job and you can't miss work." Being 'nice' is often ineffective. An ultimatum may be the catalyst needed to motivate an employee to deal with his problems. However, it is an option that should be used with care and with empathy for the employee.

In the long run, giving bleeding heart sympathy and waiving all performance standards is the worst approach. You're condoning the person's refusal to solve his problems. You're abusing others in the company by expecting them, without offering them a choice, to carry the load for this individual. Additionally, as the manager you are accountable for the success of your department or company and hence you have an obligation to the owner to protect the assets and to ensure the smooth operation of that company. Nor is it good for the individual if management is too "soft." I've never seen that work. It's far better for the employee to see the ramifications of his performance and then be given firm direction and empathetic support.

I'm not suggesting that managers be cold and cruel. I'm suggesting quite the opposite. Being overly compassionate is more beneficial to the manager than to the employee. Managers may feel good in their roles as pseudo-social workers and support people but if they really want to solve the problem, they must help employees accept personal responsibility for their own performance.

## SUMMARY POINTS

- Be sensitive to early warning signs of problems.
- Don't profess to be an expert in an area in which you are not legally qualified to practise.
- Direct people to where they can get professional help.
- Assertively enforce job performance standards. Being the nice guy isn't good management.

# STEP 21

## Guess I'm No Good!

| | | |
|---|---|---|
| Is the employee insecure, lacking self-esteem or confidence? | YES                ⟶ | Reappraise your relationship with the employee, and coach the employee. |

Two critical factors which influence an employee's motivation to do a job are self-esteem and self-confidence.

Does the employee value himself and his contribution to the company? If not, he may be insecure and lacking in self-esteem and consequently inhibited from doing good work. That pattern can happen periodically or all the way through a person's career.

An employee could be new at a job and uncertain how things should be done. As a result of her uncertainty, she might make mistakes or procrastinate. She knows how to do the job but she just isn't certain about her abilities. You could give her instructions ten times and she would likely respond that she knows how to do it, but she's really not sure. Maybe she's been pushed too far too fast. Lacking self-esteem, she really doesn't value her abilities and she has no sense of her own self-worth.

## LOSS OF SELF-ESTEEM
## IN LONG-TERM EMPLOYEES

An older employee who's been with a company for a long time may feel insecure and threatened by younger employees. He perceives the education and training of the younger employees to be superior to his own. He discounts his own experience and exaggerates theirs. In his mind, they know more, they're "computer literate" whereas he's not. They went to university and studied all sorts of things that he hasn't and so he believes they are better qualified to do the job. In fact, he can do the job perfectly well. But he begins to doubt himself because of his limited education or his age. He feels uncertain, unable to cope and incapable of adapting.

## SELF-ESTEEM IS A MATTER OF OPINION

Employees may lack self-esteem for any number of reasons. Perhaps an employee's spouse has said for years that she will never amount to much, that she isn't capable of doing much. Or perhaps the person has difficulty making friends and so suffers from low self-esteem. Maybe bosses in the past always criticized him and so now he doubts his self-worth. Or it could be the school system "did it to him." He was always told as a kid, "You're a dummy." His grades said he was a dummy so he came to believe it. As a result, he doesn't value his worth or his contribution as an employee.

One of the most important influences on every employee's self-esteem is "the boss." The relationship between the employee and the immediate supervisor has a tremendous impact on self-esteem. In fact the boss has as much if not more influence on the employee's self-esteem than the employee's own family. After a bad day at work and a confrontation with the boss, your husband or wife can try to cheer you up. But your boss just said he doesn't know why he hired you. What can a spouse or friend say that will change your boss's opinion of your worth?

## WHO WE ARE IS WHAT WE DO

It's not surprising, really, that the boss has so much impact on the employee's self-esteem.

In our Western society, who we are — our identity — is greatly determined by what we do — our job. Who we are is what we do. Test yourself. When you bump into someone you haven't seen in years, say an old schoolmate, you soon get around to asking, "Hey, what are you doing? What's your job?" In other words: "Who are you?"

The chronically unemployed often have psychiatric problems because they have difficulty coming to terms with who they are — they have no job. Society essentially tells them, "You're a nobody." You're not a member of society when you haven't got a job. Housewives used to have identity and self-esteem problems (and many still do) until society began to give due credit to the homemaker and the mother as doing "worthwhile" jobs. Likewise, househusbands are slowly finding their niche and acceptance in a society that values their contribution.

Who we are is greatly determined by the job that we do. Hence, how "good" a person we are is very greatly determined by how "well" we believe we do our work. I am a successful executive therefore I must be a successful person. Good salesperson equals good person. I am an incompetent homemaker; I question my competency as a person.

Admittedly, there is no logical or ethical link between how well we do our job and how good a person we are. But because there's such a strong connection between identity and job, this link is nevertheless established. Consequently, people who perceive failure in their jobs often have low self-esteem and low confidence.

## WHAT THE BOSS SAYS CARRIES WEIGHT

Society gives bosses the right and the obligation to assess how well employees do their jobs. A major influence on an individual's perception of how well he or she is doing a job is therefore the boss.

When the boss tells you that you are incompetent, whether you believe it or not, the words can have a significant impact on your self-esteem. Why? Because the boss is the legitimate judge of your work. Identical criticisms coming from a peer can be more readily rejected.

If you disagree with the boss's assessment, you may go home and vent your hurt, anger and frustration on the family and of course the family will be supportive because that's its role. But support from home doesn't change the fact that The Boss said you're no good.

An employee with low self-esteem may be that way because of interactions in the past with you or with former bosses. It may even be due to unintentional critical comments such as, "That's the stupidest idea I've ever heard," or "Why can't you ever get it done right?" The words may have been spoken in the heat of the moment. You really didn't mean them, but because they came from you, the boss, they will have more significance than you intended. If these kinds of comments continue, you will lower the employee's self-esteem, in turn lowering motivation and performance.

## EVERY BOSS/EMPLOYEE INTERACTION AFFECTS SELF-ESTEEM

Whenever you interact with an employee, you're doing one of three things:

maintaining the other person's self-esteem

raising it

lowering it

And once you start to lower it, intentionally or not, motivation and performance take a downhill slide.

If your problem employee appears to have low self-esteem or low self-confidence, I'm not saying that you necessarily caused it — it may be the result of years of interaction with former bosses — but because of your potential impact, you're one of the best sources to solve the problem.

## SIGNS OF LOW SELF-ESTEEM

How do you determine if the employee is lacking self-esteem? Perhaps you can tell by what she says, by the way she says it, by how she looks, by things that she does and by knowing the employee.

Indications of low self-esteem might be that the person is a social recluse, off by himself all the time, or that he is always asking for help. Perhaps the employee won't do something until he has practised it so many times it's ridiculous. Some people may be overly meticulous, wanting things explained a dozen times before they do anything. Body language and appearance also hold clues. Be careful, though, not to play amateur psychologist and deduce personality traits from any "oddities" in behavior or physical appearance. In general terms, however, extremes in any direction of behavior or appearance can be tell-tale signs. For example, insecure people may dress shabbily or be unkempt. On the other hand just the opposite could be true and not a hair will ever be out of place. You may just get a gut feeling from body language that a person doesn't take pride in herself or in her work. Or she may frequently belittle herself, blame herself too often, or just the opposite. The amount of eye contact can also be symptomatic.

## BUILDING SELF-ESTEEM

Once you assess that a person has low self-esteem, begin to address the problem by reappraising your relationship with the employee. You might be the cause of the problem. If you aren't, remember, you are part of the solution. Coach the employee. Work more closely with him, help him do the job, pick his spirits up, reinforce him in a supportive coaching relationship and begin to boost his self-esteem. Get him doing good work and reinforce that.

It may be an appropriate time to consider training or retraining the employee in certain skills. As part of this process, set up an occasion for the employee to use the skills with success — an occasion where she won't fail.

## SET UP A SERIES
## OF PSYCHOLOGICAL SUCCESSES

If you want to teach someone a difficult job, break the job into bite size chunks and let the employee learn the job a little bit at a time. Then the employee can see he's making progress and he can enjoy success and build his self-esteem. That's preferable to having an employee jump in feet first to sink or swim. Most people sink. All that they learn then is that they can't do the job.

## SOME LEARN HOW TO FAIL

Low self-esteem can be a self-fulfilling prophesy. People "know" they can't succeed and they go out of their way to prove that they're right. This condition corresponds to "learned helplessness" — a psychological phenomenon that helps explain why some people just can't be motivated. They have "learned" over the years that they are helpless and that they can't do anything to change their workplace situation.

We've all met an energetic young employee who charges in on a white horse wanting to change the world. Within a year he learns he can't change the system: "No matter what I do, I can't make any changes. They won't let me." He soon gets off his horse. He's learned not to try anymore. Why should he? He's going to fail anyway. He then sits back and lets the organization do whatever it wants because he "knows" he can't change the course of events. This phenomenon explains a lot of apparent civil service apathy. The employees work in a huge bureaucracy. They've learned that trying hard is not the way to get ahead. They decide to sit back and work at a marginal level. With this attitude, their self-esteem and self-confidence drops and consequently so does their motivation.

How do you turn this employee around? Try close supervision and lots of supportive coaching. Make sure his goals are realistic. Immediate results should not be expected however. Learned helplessness is a very resistant attitude.

---

### SUMMARY POINTS

- You may be the cause of your employee's low self-esteem.

- You are probably best able to improve your employee's self-esteem.

- Every time you interact with an employee you are maintaining, increasing or decreasing that person's self-esteem.

- Inconsequential comments and gestures by you may unintentionally erode your employee's self-esteem.

- Help your employees to experience successes, not failures.

# STEP 22

## Quit Picking On Me!

Is there a person-    YES                           Translate
ality conflict?    ————————————————→    "personality" prob-
lem into a
"behavior"
problem,
and resolve.

How many times have you been caught in the old "personality problem" trap? You've got an employee who's a real bear. He's arrogant and opinionated, a loud mouth who gets along with no one. Other people are even quitting as a result of him. But he's an excellent worker and he does his job well. Do you keep him and lose other employees or fire him and lose an excellent worker? And how can you fire him if he's doing his job so well?

Then there's the hot head in shipping who, at the drop of a hat, accuses you of picking on him whenever you ask him to realign some pallets or clean up the loading docks. He usually storms off in a huff.

The staff bicker amongst themselves. Incessantly you can hear Fern and Leslie taking verbal shots at each other and they both refuse to help each other even though it would save the department time and money.

Theoretically they're all doing their work. However personality conflicts are interfering with the smooth running of your department. What can you do?

### HERE'S THE SOLUTION

First, don't be led astray by considering only the technical aspects of the job in a job description. Social and interpersonal behaviors are also a significant part of almost every job. How people are to interact should be a requirement of job performance as well as the quality of typing, filing, welding, computing, etc. And personality — in the sense of how people behave and interrelate at work — must be dealt with. Conflicts must be confronted. Otherwise, they can disrupt a department and get in the way of people doing good work.

Therefore, don't rate the employee as a good worker if only the technical part of the job is done satisfactorily. The employee should have an obligation to interact co-operatively with others on the job and to help create a good working climate.

Second, don't deal with this type of a problem as a "personality" problem. "Personality" is just too subjective and nebulous a term. You can't reprimand or discipline people because of personality problems and you can't fire them because you don't like their attitudes. The courts won't allow it. But if people don't or won't do their jobs, you can take action. Remember, doing the job properly also includes showing appropriate social behavior.

If there is a personality conflict between the boss and the employee, who's really at fault? Why reprimand the employee? There are two people involved. Why not reprimand the boss? What you must do is translate the "personality" problem into a behavioral problem.

## DEFINE THE PERSONALITY PROBLEM
## AS A BEHAVIORAL PROBLEM

To do that, you have to decide which specific behaviors lead you to believe you have a personality conflict on your hands. What is the inappropriate behavior? Is it anti-social behavior? Is it inappropriate language directed to you as the boss? What is the employee *doing* or *saying* that causes turmoil or unrest? Then, when the inappropriate behavior is identified, deal with it. Don't try to change the person. Forget about the "personality" — you can't change someone's personality anyway.

## FOCUS ON THE OBJECTIONABLE BEHAVIOR

The employee who is always lippy with you uses language which is inappropriate to the position. Don't say, "I don't like your attitude and your personality is all wrong." Instead, say, "Look, the abusive language you're using, your abrasive tone of voice and sneering facial expression when speaking to me is inappropriate. It gets in the way of my doing my job and it's affecting your job. I want it to stop."

Other examples of inappropriate behavior might be socializing excessively on the job, discussing non-work related topics, using inappropriate language or gestures when addressing a peer or a client and refusing to assist others in work activities related to the department's function. Facial expressions can also be inappropriate, for example, that look of defiance on your employee's face annoys you every time. Whenever you ask him to do something he grimaces and pouts his lips. It's inappropriate business behavior. That's what you should be focusing on.

## YOU HAVE TO DEFINE
## WHAT MAKES BEHAVIOR INAPPROPRIATE

"Being late for work seven out of ten times, casual dress, shirt not tucked neatly into pants, shoes not shined and hair unkempt...When this happens, it lowers my confidence in assigning you special duties."

"Your pouting and brusque behavior to staff and customers is inappropriate and unprofessional." "Socializing with the staff or via the telephone while customers wait for assistance is rude."

Derisive comments made in jest, negative comments about other employees, finding fault with management but being unwilling to offer constructive criticism or to contribute at staff meetings could be symptoms of a "bad attitude." You can't directly change attitudes, but you can insist that the employee behaves in a constructive, socially acceptable manner.

When the conflict is between you and an employee, remember that the conflict is always two sided. Is there something you're doing that's causing the conflict? Is there something in your behavior that's hooking the other person's feelings? Something must be doing it. Are you interacting with the person in some way that differs from how you interact with your other employees?

Speak with the employee in question. Perhaps his perception of your "attitude" was not what you intended, or his perception of the situation was in keeping with his "laid back" attitude and carefree style. Alternatively you might ask someone else in the department to give you objective feedback. "Look, there's a conflict between me and Martha. Am I saying things I shouldn't?" But until you communicate with the employee about the problem it is unlikely that a solution can be found.

## SUMMARY POINTS

- Don't exclude "appropriate social behavior" from a job description or from performance expectations.

- What is the person *doing* that leads you to believe it is a personality problem? Deal with the inappropriate behavior.

- You can't reprimand or fire someone because of his or her "personality".

# STEP 23

## I Can't Trust Anybody!

| Does the employee distrust the company, co-workers or you, especially regarding receiving rewards for his/her good performance? | YES ⟶ | Clarify misunderstandings and expectations. |
|---|---|---|

Have you ever expected recognition but then were let down? Have you felt you earned appreciation for good work but never got any? Eventually this neglect on the part of management affects your performance.

Motivation research shows that expectation of reward contributes strongly to our degree of motivation. Our willingness to work is influenced by how strongly we believe our performance will result in a promised reward. Also, how much we're motivated today may be limited by what happened to us in the past and by what we believe will happen to us in the future.

## ASSESS THE ODDS FOR REWARD

From the employee's point of view, what are the odds of receiving rewards that the organization promises for good work? If employees think the odds are low, they won't try hard to get them.

As a manager, you may have quite a difficult time motivating your employees by promising rewards if in the past you or former managers "never came across with the goods." Potential rewards may be attractive but if the odds of getting them are low even after good performance, the result is low motivation.

## THE OLD UNATTAINABLE CARROT TRICK

An example of this phenomenon is the middle-aged employee who has been told for years, "If you do good work, keep your nose clean and don't make waves, you'll get ahead." In the employee's mind, that's what he's done — he's worked hard, he hasn't made mistakes and he's not made waves. But he doesn't get ahead, he doesn't move up the corporate ladder as a reward for good work and he doesn't see that taking place in the future. He's still in the same monotonous job and he sees friends of the boss and people coming in from outside who are promoted over his head. These rewards he perceives as not being connected with good work. As a result, his expectation for reward goes down, his motivation goes down and likewise his performance. Of course he doesn't get ahead then either. It's another self-fulfilling prophecy.

Trust is a vital part of employee motivation. If employees don't trust the boss or the company, they are not going to perform. Eventually, employees won't believe the song and dance they've been given year after year. I'm sure you've seen lots of evidence of this in different organizations. The employees are bitter toward their company and the boss. They're suspicious and they're resentful. They distrust their co-workers; they feel that their co-workers are going to steal the rewards — like recognition and the promotions — that they should be getting.

How do you discover that? By knowing the employee, talking with her, listening to what she says on the job, and watching how she acts. At times, you may have to confront her. You might ask, for instance, "What's the matter? Don't you trust me? Do you feel you've been unfairly treated?" Her lack of belief in management might not be your fault. It might have been caused over the years by others before you but it's still a legitimate problem and you have to deal with it.

## HOW TO DEAL WITH MISTRUST

If mistrust has resulted from broken promises in the past, realize you're not going to change history. Starting today, clarify your expectations of the employee by getting right to the point:

# HERMAN®

## "Here, you wanted to be plant manager. Take care of this!"

"These are my expectations and this is what you have to do to meet them." As well, clarify the employee's expectations of you: "This is what I'll deliver." Then make sure that you do. It's far better to level with the employee than to allow false expectations to sour the relationship.

Perhaps the employee has unrealistic expectations that could never be met. It is important to let him know that there's no way he's going to get that expected promotion. Tell him, "I don't have the authority to give you a promotion so don't expect it from me." It may be a bitter pill to take but it will get his feet back on the ground.

Check to see that you have not inadvertently promised things you can't deliver. How often do we find ourselves saying, "If you do this well then I'm sure you'll go far in the company" or "Your good work won't go unrecognized" or "Do this and I'll put in a good word for that new job." What the employee hears is *if* he performs well then he *will* get the promotion.

Often new managers come into their positions with high expectations and tell the gang that they're going to improve conditions for them. A year later they realize that they can't change anything — they're part of a huge bureaucracy.

It's quite common to offer rewards more attractive than we can deliver but remember that when management doesn't follow through, future motivation is destroyed.

### DELIVER REWARDS WHEN THEY ARE EARNED

In order to build your employees' trust in you as a person who gives rewards that have been earned, you will have to show by your actions that this is true. Words such as "I keep my promises" and "You can trust me" may have a hollow ring. You must show by your actions that you can be counted on.

Never set up a reward that employees know they simply can't earn. Recall the myth about performance appraisal ratings. "We don't award a ten — that means the employee is perfect." All that tells your employees is that it's futile to try hard when the reward is unattainable. Ten should be your top level of performance. You must not have a rating that you (and your employees) know you'll never give them.

Recently, a research company had a scale of one to six on its performance appraisal forms. Half jokingly, people in the company would say that, "To score a six you need two Nobel prizes." For top quality work managers awarded five and a half, saying they were really pleased with the work but they couldn't give a six. A lot of people were hurt, saying, "Well, if you can't give it, why even have it there?" If an unrealistic rating system exists in your organization, redefine your performance scale. What do you mean by top of the scale? You ought to be able to clearly enunciate what it is people will have to do to earn that top rating. It has to be achievable, and if it is achieved, the employee has to get the promised reward. If not, you are creating a pattern of distrust and diminished motivation.

Be someone who delivers the goods when the goods are earned. You will save trouble, contribute to motivation in the future and promote a more open and honest relationship right now.

---

### SUMMARY POINTS
- Never promise something to employees that you can't deliver.
- Broken promises today may destroy motivation tomorrow.
- Trust is a key factor in motivation.
- Make sure that the employee's expectations are realistic.
- Make your expectations of the employee clear.
- Recognize achievement when it is earned.

# STEP 24

## I Couldn't Care Less!

| Is the employee apathetic, un-concerned? | YES ⟶ | Increase the employee's motivation, and coach, or discipline. |

It doesn't happen often, but now and then you get an employee who is apathetic. For example, the person puts no effort into getting projects completed on time. Work drags and coffee breaks lengthen. Bare minimum performance is achieved, the employee "works to rule" and initiative is non-existent. The person couldn't care less about his work. If this description fits one of your employees, do something to increase his or her motivation.

By motivation, I mean the force needed to raise someone's level of energy and to direct and sustain behavior. This differs from "pep rally motivation" where you bring in a speaker to stimulate your employees or you hold a party or a social to make them feel appreciated.

The motivational speaker approach, while it may raise someone's level of energy and may even point behavior in some specific direction, oftentimes doesn't sustain that behavior. Similarly, after a day or two, the initial excitement of having a speaker, film, training program or social event fades away and you have to rekindle that enthusiasm. These techniques can be useful and they have their place, but they're not what I'm talking about.

What managers are looking for in the case of the apathetic employee is a process that will maintain high levels of energy. And that's what we've been looking at through all the questions of this algorithm. Almost every question relates to an aspect of motivating people.

The question "Is the employee apathetic?" is positioned at the end of the algorithm for a number of reasons. If an employee appears not to care, you can be fairly certain that the under-lying reason isn't apathy. The majority of employees want to succeed at what they do and as you work through the algorithm, you will likely discover a cause other than apathy. However if you go through all twenty-three questions and get to the end of this list, then it could be that the employee just doesn't care. It is uncommon to encounter a person who has no reason for poor performance other than apathy but your employee might be one of the few. If so, the first step is to try to increase the employee's motivation.

If your employee doesn't seem to care, then you must answer the employee's question, "What's in it for me?" Tell the employee why he or she should want to do the job properly and what the consequences will be for not performing. This is the time to make it clear to employees that if they don't do their job, they may not have a job.

## THE BOTTOM LINE

Coach your employee. Work closely with him to improve his performance and recognize and reward his good work more often. If that still doesn't motivate him, implement a formal dis-ciplinary procedure. Essentially you say, "I've done everything I can to help solve this problem: I've encouraged you to do your work, I've explained it to you, I've taught you the skills, yet you're still not taking your work seriously. I am now warning you that if you don't do this job properly, I'll take disciplinary action which could lead to your dismissal."

Discipline in such cases consists of an official warning that something unpleasant will happen if the inappropriate behavior continues. The "something" could be a verbal warning, a suspension from work for a prescribed time (usually without pay), or a discharge.

People requiring discipline will be few. Of these few, some are simply in the wrong job. Their jobs are not suited to them and they don't have the wherewithal or motivation to do something about it themselves. They sit and wait for you to do something about it. So do something. You cannot condone poor work.

## USE DISCIPLINE IN PROGRESSIVE STAGES

It's not the intent of this algorithm to give a detailed treatise on disciplinary philosophy and procedures. There are too many legal and labor/management nuances to outline one specific "way to do it." But a few general guidelines are worth emphasizing.

Of prime importance is documenting everything — time, place, details of poor behaviors, witnesses, warnings of future repercussions, disciplinary action — in essence a history of the employee's performance and your interactions. The procedure, while tedious, will probably be very helpful to you should you be asked to explain or defend your actions.

Discipline should be used in progressive stages, from mild to severe. Usually, four stages are used.

### 1. Verbal Warning

For minor offences, the employee should be given a verbal warning to stop the offending behavior. This warning should be noted in the employee's personnel file. If this does not correct the situation within a reasonable length of time, proceed to stage 2.

### 2. Written Warning

The employee should be given a formal written warning indicating in detail the offence, your reason for concern and the consequences if he or she does not stop the offending behavior (usually a suspension for a prescribed period of time without pay). One copy of this warning should be given to the employee, and one copy entered in his or her personnel file. If this measure does not correct the situation, proceed to stage 3.

### 3. Suspension

The employee should be suspended from work for a prescribed period of time as determined by contract agreements, precedents, the seriousness of the offence, or the employee's work record. This disciplinary action must be the same as that forewarned in the previous written warning. At this time the employee is warned in writing that further misbehavior could result in discharge.

### 4. Discharge

Should the behavior continue following the suspension, discharge the employee or suspend the employee without pay pending final discharge. Note that you need not go through all four stages. Discipline may begin at any stage depending upon the seriousness of the offence. Also, you may repeat any of the first three stages when appropriate, as long as the discipline is commensurate with the offence committed and consistent with past practice and precedent and as long as the employee has been warned.


## THE RED HOT STOVE ANALOGY

Picture a red hot stove and a little girl playing nearby. Her mother warns her not to touch the stove because it is very hot and she will be burned. The child disregards her mother and touches the stove. Instantly, she is burned and she runs away crying. Four discipline principles in this short scenario also apply in the workplace.


### 1. Advance Warning

The mother warned the little girl what would happen if she touched the stove. Discipline must *always* be preceded by a clear warning. Surprise discipline is unfair and of little value. The goal is to encourage the employee to perform satisfactorily by using the *threat* of discipline not by using the discipline itself.


### 2. Immediate Discipline

As soon as the girl touched the stove she was burned. Likewise, at work, discipline should immediately follow the improper behavior. Delaying the discipline may be interpreted as "getting even."


### 3. Consistency

Every time the girl touches the hot stove, she will be burned. In business, every time a rule is broken, some price must be paid. Inconsistent discipline is unjust and will result in valid grievances. From a psychological perspective, failure to consistently enforce regulations will encourage insubordination and increase disciplinary problems.

## 4. Impersonal Rules

If the girl's mother touches the hot stove, she will be burned too. Rules apply to the act, not to the individual. At work, the same principle applies. Individual circumstances such as intent, seniority and previous work history need to be taken into account. But if an individual breaks a rule, some price has to be paid by that individual. Above all, if discipline is to be an effective deterrent, management *must ensure* that rules of conduct and associated penalties are known and understood by all. In public, ignorance of the law is no excuse for breaking it but at work, management's failure to educate can be a valid reason for overruling a company's attempt to discipline. Merely distributing policy manuals to new employees or posting notices on a bulletin board are insufficient measures for educating the work force. Employees should be *taught* the rules, regulations and standards that management wants to enforce.

In brief summary, sometimes you have to take the employee to the brink before he or she realizes that you are serious about work performance. In these instances, discipline can be a very positive force and possibly your last alternative. If necessary, use it, but use it correctly and document everything.

---

### SUMMARY POINTS

- A fair question for all to ask is, "What's in it for me if I do good work?"

- Some people have to see the unpleasant consequences of their unacceptable work before they take the job seriously.

- Plan for discipline very carefully, give lots of warning to the employee, do it fairly and objectively and document everything.

# STEP 25

## Enough's Enough!

If you've been through steps 1 to 24, then you're probably
being led down the garden path. Forget diagnosing the
reasons and just enforce the performance standards.
Consider discipline.

If you finally arrive at question 25 and you still haven't figured
out what the cause of the problem is, you're probably on a
wild-goose chase.

You've given it a good try. You've explored a long list of
valid, common and not so common reasons for poor performance and yet you still can't figure out why this employee won't
or can't do the job.

Don't analyse the situation to death. If you have explored
all the issues raised in questions 1 to 24, then you've considered
whether the person has the skills, the direction, the incentives,
the performance standards and the feedback to do the job.
Everything is taken care of from a management point of view.
Forget about diagnosing any further.

It's time to be a firm, assertive boss. This means you should:

1. Make it explicitly clear to the employee what is expected
   of him or her.

2. Tell the employee what the performance standards are.

3. Tell the employee what his or her obligations are as an
   employee.

4. Enforce the performance standards.

5. Discipline the employee if he or she won't comply with
   the standards.

# The Final Word

From managers I frequently hear, "My people aren't doing their jobs. They're just not working out. What can you *do to them* to get them back on track?" Using all the diplomacy possible I have to answer, "If the employee is not performing, he must be managed better, and that's what you, the boss, have to do.

Review the algorithm and what do you see? Almost all the causes of performance problems relate back to the boss or the organization — unclear directions, poor employee selection, no feedback, poorly designed jobs, inappropriate or ill-timed rewards and punishments, inadequate training, false promises, etc. Most problems with the workforce are *caused by management.*

Review the suggested solutions on the right side of the algorithm and you'll see that all solutions describe what management is to do. The solutions to all employee performance problems rest with management. It would be nice if employees solved their own problems, and often they do, but ultimately management must take the responsibility to see that problems are resolved. If you manage people then *you're* the solution (and frequently the cause) of any performance problem. Why? Because your job is to select, direct, lead, motivate and coach your employees.

It may be difficult to accept, but if your employee isn't working out, first ask — What am I doing wrong? Where have I failed? What should I be doing differently? Use the algorithm and the answer is often simple.

Remember, when the problem is solved and the employee's performance improves, much of the credit should go to you. The employee is working better because you're managing better. With luck your boss will recognize this and your performance will be rewarded. But that's another story!